LEARN FROM MY MISSTEPS

TRINESHA CATRELL

Copyright 2022 by Trinesha Catrell

Holy Bible, New International Version®, NIV® Copyright ©1973, 1978, 1984, 2011 by Biblica, Inc.® Used by permission. All rights reserved worldwide
Holy Bible, New International Version

All rights reserved. Any unauthorized reprint or use of this material is prohibited. No part of this book may be reproduced or transmitted in any form or by any means electronic or mechanical including photocopying, recording, or by any information storage and retrieval system without express written permission from the author.

Disclaimer: While all attempts have been made to verify the accuracy of the information provided in this publication the author assumes no responsibility for any errors or omissions. Should the reader face any outward website difficulties it is recommended they seek out professional technical support. to rectify the same. The author will not be held responsible for any repercussions beyond the scope of this book.

Contents

Introduction
....1

Chapter 1
A Childlike Mind..5

Chapter 2
If I Only Knew, If I Knew Back Then What I Knew Now..11

Chapter 3
Attraction..31

Chapter 4
Know It All..37

Chapter 5
Lust Looks a Lot like Love..................................43

Chapter 6
Tragic Comfort 57

Chapter 7
Codependency 61

Chapter 8
Losing Myself..67

Chapter 9
Finding My Purpose *89*

Chapter 10
Becoming Independent *97*

Chapter 11
Gaining My Independence ………….........................….*105*

Chapter 12
Independent…….…...…….....................................……*119*

Chapter 13
Interdependent……...…....…..................................……*141*

Chapter 14
Emotional trials..…*149*

Chapter 15
Out of my hands.....………….....................................…*153*

Chapter 16
Closure……………….…..…...*161*

Conclusion.. **173**
Book club..**181**

My Quote..**185**

Introduction

Can we get a proper vetting check in order before we even decide to be in a relationship? If you are like me, you thought you had it all figured out and didn't take the time to properly vet your partner before deciding to be in a relationship.

You may have thought you were grown, and you got this, but true growth and a part of being grown is acknowledging your flaws and learning as much as you can in any situation/ conversation/ life event/ tragedy.

A year ago, I could not tell you who I could have even imagined that I would be. I was so confused, no wonder my marriage fell apart. Oh, maybe that was too deep to talk about my failed relationship so soon, but I am the type of person who is an open book and wears her heart on her sleeve. Before I might have been ashamed of that, but this is who I am. This is who God created me to be. I am not ordinary, but extraordinary and so are you.

Can we stop settling for the fly guy because people who settled did not know there was more than that in life? What about the job that we hate to go to, but blame everyone else and everything else for the reason we cannot go further in life? How about we stop blaming our past, family, friends, and circumstances for our life. We are better than that and can do ANYTHING and when I say anything I mean ANYTHING we set our mind to. Imagine anything you ever wanted, and you CAN have it.

My why: I do not want ANY other woman/man to go through what I went through. I experienced that feeling of loss when the person is still alive. That feeling of having a piece of your soul being ripped out of your body is unlike any physical pain that I have ever felt in my entire life.

Follow me through my journey so we can break some low standards and start standing for something.

"He performs wonders that cannot be fathomed, miracles that cannot be counted."

Job 5:9

Chapter 1
A Child-like Mind

As a child at the age of 8, I felt like I fit in. I laughed and played without a care in the world, that is until one day when my choice to stay a child was taken away from me.

That day that I lost my opportunity to choose, I lost my confidence and my childlike spirit. I felt like a feather in the wind aimlessly floating around. I could not figure out who I was anymore.

When I was little, I never really noticed a difference between myself or anyone else. It wasn't until someone mentioned something like my complexion, or their father, or my mannerisms that I was even able to decipher a difference. I always knew there was something I was here for even at an early age.

Playing on the swing set and running in the yard seemed to come naturally, but when it came to making friends, I could never really fit in. I felt like everyone I met could see my backstory of everything that I have endured through me. I became obsessed with being attracted to someone. If I was in a store, in school, or anywhere I picked someone that I liked and then fixated on it. I know now that this is so wrong and what I should have done is get some help right then but give me a break I was only a child. Having a crush was the only form of normalcy that I felt. It was the only thing that I felt like I had control over as if choosing who I wanted gave me some sort of power.

I would set goals, but I did not set standards in school or my career. I did when it came to relationships with others whether that be a friendship or a significant other. I never stuck with what I wanted. When it came to my career I would get a job, but never go for a promotion. I would get offered promotions, but I never took the initiative.

As a child, I always liked scary movies because I knew a dark truth that as a kid, I would have never considered a reality. The dangers parents protect their children from I never got the chance to experience in the way protected children had experienced it. I wish that I could have enjoyed being a child a little while longer.

Most of the time I rushed through life. I wanted to be grown so badly I did not take the time necessary to be a child. To grow and learn everything I could at every age. What happened to me felt wrong, but it was as if I could not pinpoint what was wrong with it. If you are like me sex was not something that was brought up at all in the household. I wish I could have had that talk growing up. Maybe if I had learned the difference between good touch and bad touch, I would have known what happened was not right and I would have known that I have/ had a right to say no. I had a right to tell someone. I wanted to tell someone, but I was too afraid, and I blamed myself. I was the one that agreed to go there. I was the one who wanted to be included. I wanted to feel like I fit in. I just wanted to play a game, not have my choice taken from me. I had a right to not blame myself. I had an opportunity to be who I was and embrace who I was.

I got the opportunity to talk to the person and they apologized and said that it was not my fault. The guilt that I didn't even realize that was that I was harboring was released at that instant. I felt something break off me that I didn't even realize was still a part of me.

Silence can create a cycle of toxicity that can become the norm. You have a choice in life no matter what happened in your past. Stand up for who you are and be proud of who you are.

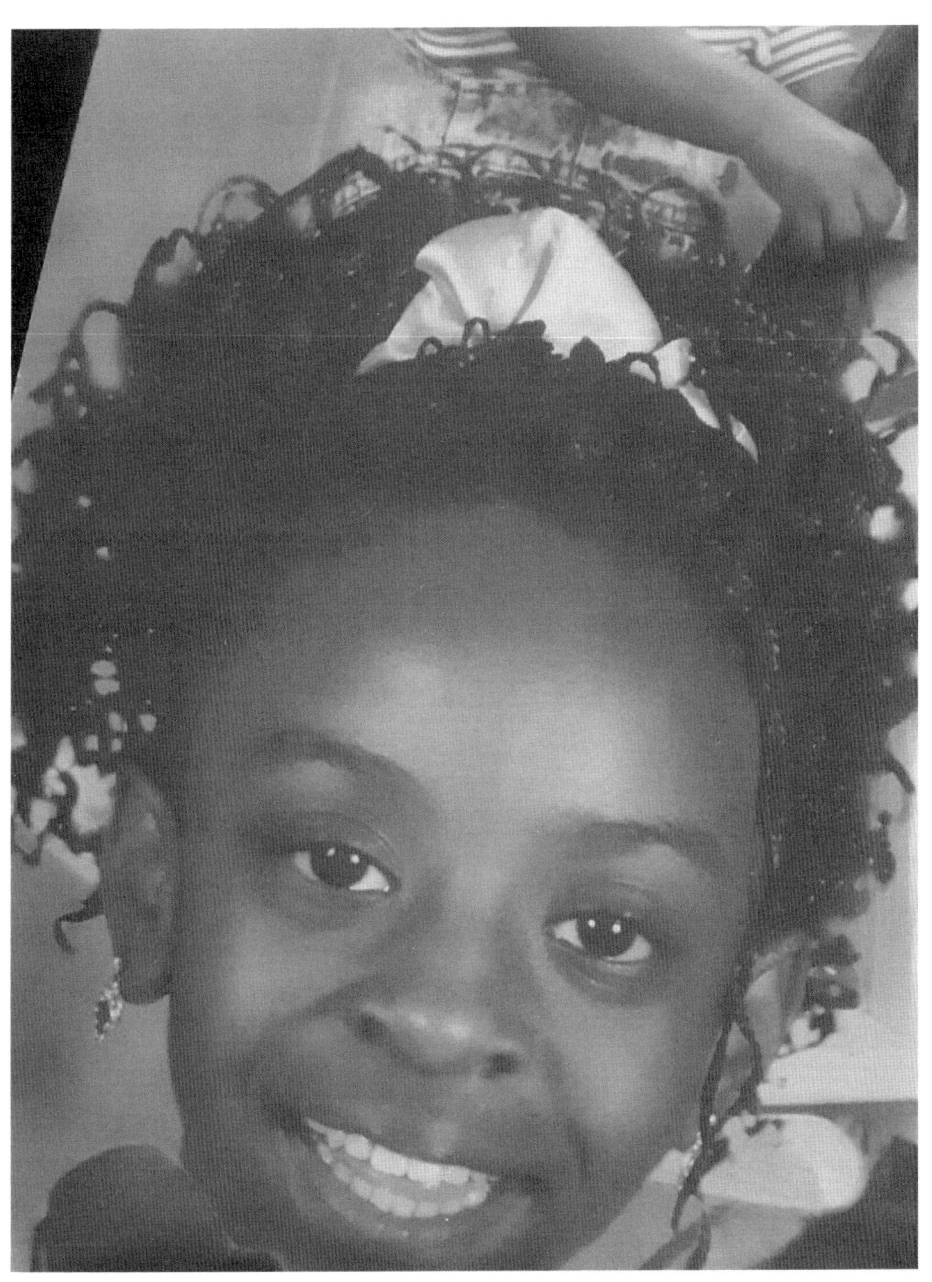

"Do not be misled, bad company corrupts good character." 1 Corinthians 15:33

Chapter 2
If I Knew Back Then What I Know Now

Even at an early age, I tried to figure out my purpose. Why was I here? I always felt misunderstood. I wanted to express myself, but my voice was gone. I was so angry. I never understood why.

In school, I remember a teacher asking me to write a letter. In this letter, the teacher said that I had to pick one person and the entire world that was inspirational and meant the most to me. This letter had to be five sentences long and it had to be something that was important to me. As I sat down getting ready to write the letter the first person that popped into my head was my mom. I do not remember all the words in the letter that I was asked to write but I do remember a few key things that really stand true even to this day. I wrote my mom is amazing and she is the person that I look up to. She has been there for me every day of my life and is one of the strongest people I have ever known. One day I hope to be like her. The word for word of this letter that I just reiterated may not be precise, but you get the gist of it. It is so important to keep in mind what is important in your life and make that a priority and not make having a crush a priority. I remember going through school and I noticed that some of the other kids were starting to develop, and I was flatter than a board when it came to the chest area. I did not feel like I was missing out on anything, but I could see the attention that some of the other girls were getting when as they were developing, and I was not. I did not feel any jealousy towards them I just knew that I wanted to fit in and that I had to fit in. So, one day when I was in 5th grade super young in elementary school, I decided I am going to stuff my bra. I felt ridiculous and it only lasted from the bathroom to the classroom and before I knew it there were tissues falling out of the top of my shirt out of the bottom of my shirt and I just pretended like I was blowing my nose it was the most hilarious thing ever. So, I guess we could say that that did not last long at all. I had friends in elementary school and one friend that I met when I was in first grade, her name was Veronica. We met one day when I went to school, I entered the classroom. We were wearing the exact same purple sweatsuit. It felt good to feel like I could relate to someone and have a friendship based on commonality. When we both looked at each other and we had the same outfit on, and I just could not believe we were wearing the same thing and we were both very excited. From that day all the way through middle school and even some high school we were the closest of friends. As I started middle school things started to change a little. I started to become a little more self-conscious. I knew I wasn't going to be that type of girl that was doing things with other people or boys, but

I knew that I needed to do something to get other people's attention I just did not know what it was going to be.

One day in 6th grade I remember the whole school being quiet and there being a lockdown. There must have been something serious that was going on for us to have to sit in our classrooms. We had the VHS tape and the radio station playing. There had been an attack on the twin towers. As a kid I had no idea what was going on, but I knew that it was something super serious. There were lockdowns at schools, there were lockdowns at a bunch of different important buildings, and I just did not know how extreme or what was happening. We sat in the classroom and listened as we heard about the plane crashing into the twin tower. They were shouting out several casualties. So many people lost their lives that day. It is so weird how something this big that happens in your life can stay with you for the rest of your life. I remember exactly where I was, who the teacher was, and exactly where I was in the classroom. I was in 6th-grade in my English class with my teacher Ms. Bradshaw at the desk by the window. It was a dejected day. I remember going home and asking my grandmother what happened and why someone would do something like that. She stated that she did not know then you could really see the somber looks on everyone around me. My heart goes out to all of those families who were affected by such a tragic event. Cherish the things and the people that you have in your life.

****

    Later that year there was a rumor going around school that I stuffed my bra it was completely hilarious because I had just stuffed my bra the year before for maybe 30 minutes if that. It was also hilarious to me that they could think that, and I barely had a visible chest that any person could see from 2 feet in front of me let alone a mile away. I went on to tell those kids that it was not true, but you know when a rumor starts you cannot really stop it until the next thing comes along. By the end of 6th grade, I ended up having my menstrual cycle at my cousin's house. I had ridden the bus there for the last week of school. We were just having fun laughing and the next thing you know I just had this like attraction to this one person that I had never had before. I had recognized things were attractive or unattractive, but I did not feel like this before, so it was a little weird. I thought I was going to die. But it was just my period. I was so embarrassed at my cousin's house because no one told me what this thing was. I was literally sitting in the bathroom and talking to my cousin and her mother through the door asking her what I should do. My aunt went on to call my grandmother and my mother and let them know what had happened. At first, I thought I was in trouble I had no idea what I was doing I had no idea what was wrong, and I initially thought oh my gosh it is because I had feelings for this boy that I must have damaged something in my mind or my body. But I had no idea that this was just a normal part of life and that a menstrual cycle just happens it was not something that you do or do not do it is just hormonal. My cousin's mom went on to describe to me what was happening and tell me that it was completely normal. She handed me a few pads and closed the door. My cousin and I ended up talking and we just played games, but I was not as comfortable as I usually was. It was weird. I talked to her about what was happening, and she said oh yeah you know I've had mine since 3rd grade or whatever grade it was and of course, I had no idea what I was doing. I was so happy that it was the last week of school, and I did not have to worry about this until school started again. At that age, it is so weird because you feel like you are so grown up, but you are still a child, so you are trying to figure out who you are and get that independence while still trying to fit in. I wanted to be everything that I saw on TV, but I felt like I was starting to see myself more. I was starting to think about what I had and what I did not have. At this age, I was not playing softball anymore which was my escape. Softball was a thing that everyone in my family did. Just having the ball in my hand and being able to release it and throw it with all my might and releasing all of that negative energy that I held inside of my body was so peaceful. I could release anything that was on my mind that I did not have to worry about when I was in a baseball game. I could hit the ball, feel the bat in my hands, the metal bat electrifying my

fingers, and all of the negative energy flow out of my body as the bat hit against the ball moving it throughout the field. I could feel all of the stress in my body release it so when I ran from base to base and slid to home plate. Baseball was
the thing that gave me the most peace. It was the thing that made me feel like I fit in like I finally had found something that belonged to just me that was not something that anyone else could take away from me or so I thought. It was not long before I had been asked to be an All-Star. An All-Star team was a softball team made up of all the best players on all the different teams and they would play in nationals or around various places in the state. I wanted to be a part of that team so badly but having a conversation with my grandmother she pointed out that I would be outside in the sun and that I would have to worry about getting darker. At that age I did not really care about my complexion. I did not care about what I looked like outside I just knew that I was having the best time of my life, I was somewhere where I felt like I belonged, and this was something that I

really enjoyed doing. I knew that baseball was something that every person in my family did and they all enjoyed it as well. It was something that kind of kept me feeling like a part of the family. I always felt different even from an early age. I knew that I wanted to belong. I wanted to be someone who people would see as someone. I did not know exactly what it was that I was looking for, but baseball gave me a twinge of hope. As I moved throughout middle school even after the period, I learned that sometimes when we want to fit in it does not mean that we have to fit in. I at this time had already started noticing boys. Wrong move. I had a crush on this one guy, and I decided to say that I would have sexual relations with him if he was my boyfriend because I felt like being in a relationship with someone would allow me to fit in somewhere. I thought that if I was with someone who everyone else thought was cool then maybe people would think that I belong there, and I would not stand out as much as I had been. So, here is the thing about saying that you are going to do something with a guy that you do not intend on doing anything with. Eventually, the person will ask you if you are going to do it. Me being that young I just thought I could just say things and not do anything, and it would just be fine. Needless to say, eventually he broke up with me because I was not willing to do those things and I was fine with that. I decided that me and my two other closest friends were going to all remain virgins until we met someone that we truly were in love with. I felt like if I was not going to fit in, I was going to do something that was different. I did not know if this was a good or a terrible thing, I just knew that this was something in my heart that I felt like I needed to do. By the time I reached 7th-grade things started to change. I started getting bullied by this guy named Robert. Robert was a short guy who all the other girls in school liked. They thought he was so handsome and so funny because he had all the best jokes. I on the other hand was not that attracted to Robert. I noticed that he was attractive, but he was not the type of person that I wanted to be with. I do not know what it was that made me feel that way but at that age, I just knew that he was not my person. I felt like there was something off about him. Some people do not like it when you reject them. So, because I did not pay him as much attention as all of the other girls, he ended up bullying me. Every day he would say every mean thing that he could possibly think of. He would say every dark-skinned joke that you have ever imagined anything that you can look up online is probably what you called me. felt like the only reason I was on earth was to be a target for everyone to dump all their insecurities on. My biological father was insecure about being a father and it made me feel alone and like I had to protect myself because he was not there. I thought that everyone would leave. Had I known then to appreciate the people that really wanted to be in my life like my stepdad who is the best father that anyone could ask for I would have saved myself years of hurt and disappointment. My friends at school were not my friends. My bully was insecure because I did not like him in that way. I could feel all their insecurities and hate all over me. I could feel it taking over my mind.

When I would try to have a good day, I could feel the world pulling against me. I wanted to believe in myself, but at that age, it felt impossible. I would start confident with my head held high and then the first insult would come and another and another. With every insult, I could feel my confidence and hope dwindling. Every day I could feel my spirit growing lower and lower. I wanted to believe the insecurities about myself that I had never even thought of before the insults. Every day at school made me feel increasingly depressed. Whenever I got home from school I finally got away from my bully. I would watch a television show or a movie so I could escape my life. I focused on all the things that were wrong in my life instead of the many blessings that I was given. If I had looked at the blessing that I had in my life I would have noticed all the people who were there for me and that I had everything that I needed. You can do anything you believe you can do. I know it seems cliche, but that is what sets the ordinary apart from the extraordinary.

My self-esteem started to die. I had friends but none of my friends were brave enough to stand up for me besides three other young women that I went to school with. When I was in class one day these three girls stood up for me. Their names were Shameka, Ashley, and Caitlin. Shameka was dark-skinned like me, but no one ever picked on her and she had the most beautiful eyes that you could ever imagine they were like a Hazel some sort of distinct color. Ashley was extremely popular she had been raised by both her mother and father and she was of Indian descent. Her hair was so gorgeous, so shiny, and flawless. She had the body that almost every guy would say was amazing and she had the manners of someone who was raised really well. Her personality was everything. Caitlin was gorgeous as well blonde hair blue eyes the total package. She was a black belt in karate, and she always kept to herself. She never started an argument with anyone, but she stood up for me that day and I really appreciate those girls for doing that. They have no idea how much that meant to me. It was only two days out of my whole 7th and 8th-grade career that I can even imagine having any peace from my bully. The time that those three wonderful strong young women stood up for me and the day that Ms. Hammer played the video about bullying in the school on the VHS tape back in the day. Hopefully, I am not aging myself too much by telling this story. Ms. Hammer put in this VHS tape, and it displayed this kid who was constantly getting bullied. He could not take it anymore and he decided to end things. At the end of the video, I felt like finally there was a way out. I looked over at my bully who looked at me with pleading eyes. He looked like he wanted to say that he was sorry, but he was too afraid to speak up in front of everyone else. For that whole week, I had peace. He didn't say anything mean to me he was nice to me. One day when I went over to my aunt's house, we even watched the movie together. There was nothing crazy or weird that happened, but we just laughed at the movie and then just talked about school stuff. It was pretty cool to see him as actual human being and not someone that was trying to ruin my life.

When I played softball, practiced, or was around the team I did not even think about boys at all. I got to spend time with my grandmother and my friends, and I felt like I belonged. Sometimes I think back and wonder if I had continued to play through the recreational center and college, but I doubted myself so much that I knew I would have eventually given up. I felt like I was never good enough and everyone felt sorry for me. I thought that was the reason that I was selected for the All-Stars.

When I got to middle school, I had the option to try out for the team and play softball. I did not even try. I kept telling myself that I was not enough and will never be enough. I told myself, "I would only embarrass myself." I thought I will just get darker if I play in the hot sun. At that moment I wish I could have believed in myself and that I would not have worried about getting darker. Who cares how dark I am.? Now I love my brown skin. Why couldn't I love myself? I was worthy of being a part of a team. I was/am enough.

By the end of my 8th grade school year, my grandmother and mother were talking about moving me to another school since I had to deal with a bully for two years of my middle school career. My mom decided that she was ready to move me to another school district. I was devastated about leaving behind the friends that I thought I did have, but I also understood why I had to leave. I cried and cried and cried for so long because I knew that I would not see my friends like I had previously saw them. Veronica and I hugged at our graduation, and we cried because we knew that we were going to miss each other. I knew that we would see each other again but it was just the fact that we would be going to two totally different schools, and I would not be going to sleepovers at her house every weekend or every other weekend. It was also the fact that I knew that some things were going to change and as a kid change is pretty scary.

  I started looking for anything that made me fit in. I wanted to join sports but could not do any extracurricular activities. Eventually, I began playing volleyball and felt like I was part of a team. After the opening season, I played for the season. I wanted to be a part of a team, but I was not good at volleyball. Before this point, I knew I was brown-skinned, and I heard a lot of other light-skinned people talk about how they did not want to become darker. As for me, I thought about my completion, but I did not care what complexion I was. I just wanted to be a part of a team that would be doing something that everyone in my family had done.

You are enough. Believe in yourself. The only person/ thing that stands in your way is you. God has given you everything that you need; you just need to go for it. Every doubtful thought you have you must nip it in the bud. As soon as doubt crosses your mind think of 2 good things about yourself. I call this the 2 to 1. Every negative thought in your life takes 2 things that will allow your spirit to clear it away. You can say 2 affirmations, 2 accomplishments, and/or 2 scriptures. This will be exactly what you need to create a successful mind and we all have it inside of us.

    A lot of my trauma turned to anger. I was short tempered and harbored hate in my heart. I was so angry most of the time. I did not know why I was so angry. I had a family member who told me as a child I needed to be in a psych ward or a farm because of the anger I harbored. When I was 12 years old, I had no idea where that anger stem from. I think her comment was meant for protection, but it felt like an attack against me and not for me. I wish I would have had been sent to a counselor instead of being ashamed and criticized. I went on believing for over a decade that I was the only problem.

This is not to beat up on my family members but to bring awareness. I know that she helped the best that she could, but our mistake may help another child of God.

My hope is that this helps other children or family members see that they need help not negative criticism. Maybe now that self-care and seeing a psychologist have become more normal more parents would be willing to get the necessary help for their children. Going to a therapist would have allowed me to express myself in an unbiased space and even realize that what happened to me was not my fault. This would have saved me years. What the devil uses for evil God can use for good so in essence, my story can help someone in my situation know that it's not their fault, it is not your fault, and seeking help does not mean that you are the problem.

"Taking the forbidden fruit from the garden."

Genesis 3:6

Chapter 3

Attraction

As I started my new school year my mom did my hair and we picked out several outfits. My grandmother also took me shopping with her friend from work and her daughter. We had so much fun going on our back-to-school shopping trips to the Potomac Mills Mall.

When it came time for school to start, I was so nervous. I had no idea how I was going to make friends. I did not know if this was just going to be a repeat of my previous school or if I was going to all of a sudden become popular, in my dreams. I did not know what to expect at all. On my first day at school, I recognized that one of the girls from my old middle school was at that school with me her name was Kira. Kira was one of my closest friends at the beginning of my high school career. We were talking about the old school and how the new school was different. We talked about the population, the mannerisms, and the diverse ways that people use slang and talk. I made other friends within the first month of school that pretty much stuck with me throughout my entire high school career.

Two of those friends were my friend Kay and JoJo. Kay and I met one day in English class when the class was split into two and they formed a study group for vocabulary aside from the normal lesson plan. We just started talking like we were old friends. Kay is the type of friend that you can tell anything to, and it ends with her. She is very understanding and caring. I do not have to pretend to be anything but myself when I am around her. She is the type of person who believes in standing up for others. I could vent, laugh, cry, and everything in between. JoJo is the type of friend who is protective. You know that friend whom any problem you have will back you no matter what. Do not get it twisted she will tell you when you are wrong in the most loving way while still supporting your stance. She is a great listener and completely selfless, beautiful, and so smart. Her communication is top-level. When you have friends like that, you hold on to them. In fact, we are still good friends to this day. No matter where I am in my life or where they are in their life, we always make sure that we are intentional about reaching out to check on each other.

Think of all the billionaires or successful people. What do they have in common? They had a great circle, and a dream or a project that they believed in even before it came to fruition. Stop doubting yourself and thinking yes of course that happened to them because they are special. You are special. We all are given gifts and things that would change the world as we know it. Whether that be a product or a person like a child. Your child could be destined for greatness. I used to think there could only be one person and a friend group or family that was talented or could be successful, but we all have it inside of us.

We all can be /get better and better each day. Who cares if you need the practice to perfect your gift? You are worth it, and you can do and achieve anything you put your mind to. Our children need to see us succeed, our parents need to see us succeed, our grandparents need to see us succeed, our colleagues need to see us succeed, our friends need to see us succeed, and even our enemies need to see us succeed. And that is not to say that we are going to rub it in our enemies' faces, but this way they can know that they can do and achieve greatness as well.

No one person is better than another person we are all human. The only difference between the two of us is our ability to never give up. Each day will not be rainbows and butterflies but take every terrible experience and negate it by thinking of something good. Character means more than attraction! Do not let your wants guide your decision. You got this.

"But I say, walk by the Spirit, and you will not gratify the desires of the flesh." Galatians 5:16

Chapter 4

Know It All

I do not know about you, but when I was younger, I thought I knew everything. I would hear adults say things like I wish I were younger, and I would think why when you can do whatever you want. If only it was that easy. I did not get to have any real talks about relationships and why you should do what needed to be done and do what you needed to do. I always took advice as a suggestion instead of a guideline. I had seen other relationships around me, but I never got the concept of conflict resolution or how to effectively communicate. I always felt like something was wrong with me and I never quite fit in. I had a friend with whom it seemed like we would always compete. I would try to be supportive but every time I felt a twinkle of hope or like I could do this she would take it away. I understood we were friends, and we would like the same things but sometimes it was more of an anything you can do I can do better. I used to love to sing but gave it up for her. I felt so low. I felt like why I tried to compete when she would always win. If there was a guy that liked me, she would say you know he always hit on me or he wants me, and I would never talk to that guy again. It felt disgusting to even think about liking a guy that she was interested in. I was throwing away guys like it was a game of Hot Potato. That is until it came to my ex. He seemed like the only guy that she did not have a back story for. I was so overprotective of our relationship we did not spend time together and when we did, I always made sure he was not around. I was 18 years old, and Xavier told me that my friend reached out to him online. It really hurt my feeling and my friendship with Veronica. I was livid because why would not she believe me when I told her that we were together and why would she reach out to him and not tell me. I did not confront her I just distanced myself further and further. One day we stopped talking to each other altogether. I would think of her from time to time and wish I would have known enough to dive deeper and ask more questions. It seemed like I knew everything but how to do that. Everything seemed fine until the social media thing and her and my cousin started to hang out increasingly more and I started to feel left out because they stopped including me and started treating me like an enemy instead of a comrade.

Sometimes I think about the friendship we had and how I wish we could have spent more time loving each other instead of competing. If could go back, I would apologize for not coming to her to tell her how I felt about everything. It was as if I never gave her the chance to respect my feelings or let me down. I was so afraid of being hurt and losing one of my first relationships ahead outside of my family. From 9 years old to 23 we were friends, and a 13-year-old friendship was gone, and I thought I was protecting myself. If I did make the right decision, I handled it very poorly. It felt like I was her only competition and if she could beat me, it gave her the energy that she needed. It was hard because I really took up for her and wanted to remain friends then. The best thing I should have done was reach out and respectfully voice my opinion. Maybe then I could have made an educated decision regarding our friendship. Moving forward that is exactly what I will do.

    In my first year in college, I took a psychology class that talked about the id, ego, and superego. This is like the cartoons a lot of us would watch as we grew up that show the devil on one shoulder and the Angel on the other shoulder. This theory was introduced by Sigmund Freud. Sometimes it is easier to think that your side is the only one that matters without taking into consideration the consequences. If you are ever in an unfortunate situation, take the time to talk it over with the other person whether that be a friend partner, job, or family member. You will be amazed how communication can change the narrative of the entire situation.

"When Naomi was mourning the death of her husband and 2 sons." Ruth 1:3

Chapter 5
Lust looks a lot Like Love

In March 2005 of my 9th-grade career I met this guy named Xavier. Xavier was one of the coolest guys in school. He was handsome, smart, charismatic, charming, and everything a girl could ever ask for in 9th grade.

We met in the hallway as I was walking toward my class. He asked to walk me to class. The next day I was at my locker talking to one of my friends named Jim. My other friends said that Jim wanted to ask me something but was interrupted by Xavier. I later learned that Jim wanted to ask me out. Xavier exclaimed, "why are you talking to my girlfriend?" I said oh I am your girlfriend and he said yes and then I said OKAY. How crazy is it that I would not even know this guy and just decide okay I am just going to date him. I did not even consider who he was what he was about. All I knew about him was that he was very handsome and that he was immensely popular. At the time I felt like this was what was most important. He would walk me to my classes every day and carry my books. He would treat me with so much respect. We would talk to each other every day after school and stay on the phone extremely late. We even fell asleep on the phone many times. Xavier would walk me from the bus in school in the morning, to the bus when I would get out of school, and to class. He would be either on the stairs waiting for me or waiting for me by the double doors by the entrance. I managed to stay focused on my schoolwork but all of a sudden, I felt like Xavier was something that I had been missing. Everything seemed to be going great until one day when Xavier said I love you. I said I love you too. It was one of the first times that any guy had ever said that he loved me. I thought that this was what I had been waiting for.

In school we felt like we were dating for years but, it was only an abbreviated time. After I said I love you I told myself that I wanted to remain a virgin and the only thing that would make me change my mind was if I knew for sure that I was in love. I know I had never felt the way I felt with Xavier before. I told Xavier I wanted to see him. One day I decided that I was ready. Xavier and I decided to try to sneak out together. Everything seemed fine and I did have some second thoughts, but I also did not know what to expect. I did not know who I was, and I felt like everyone else had already been having sex and I was the only person who was left. I felt like well at least this is a guy that I actually love and not just some random guy. I thought that Xavier was actually a good guy that was until I decided to give myself to him. Once I did that everything changed. He started to become annoyed on telephone calls. He started to look at me differently. I could feel him judging me like I was not the person that he thought that I was because I decided to do this. Before I knew it our phone calls were not lasting as long. I would be more angry about things that really did not matter to me. I could feel less attention from him. The next thing you know there were rumors whirling around the school. All of these guys had known that I had had sex. I didn't tell anyone so I knew Xavier was the one that told everyone. There were people coming up to me asking me if it was true and I said no but I lied. I did not want anyone to know the mistake that I made. In art class a few guys asked me if I was a virgin. I said yes and they laughed in my face. I talked to one of the guys alone and he said Xavier told him that I was no longer a virgin. I was so mad and embarrassed. How could he do that to me? And this is the moment I should have walked away. I thought I should not have done it in the first place. He said that he was happy and excited because it was his first time as well. I said even if it was that was not right that you told anyone. I stayed mad for a few days till a week, and we continued to stay in our relationship. I wanted to prove that I had made the right decision I wanted for our relationship to last forever. I thought that what I did was the right decision. I was in such a rush at that age to be a grown up, but I felt like I had to prove something to myself. I wanted to feel like I belonged. I wanted to feel like I was good enough. I wanted to feel like I was enough even though I was bullied in middle school that no one would ever bully me again because I was cool now. And I am not saying that because I want you to think that I did this because I wanted to be cool because having sex never makes you cool it just makes you easy. I just felt like I was on another level and there were other girls who were not on that level. I felt like because I had sex and he said that he loved me that that would be enough to keep us together forever. How stupid is that? I was the type of girl in middle school in all of my life who never put up with anything I had standards. I believed in myself, and I allowed some guy that I barely even knew to change my entire perspective. I would love to say that that is where the relationship ended but it is not. I continue to put up with Xavier's dismissive behavior in his missing time I felt like because I gave myself to him that I could never face anyone else because I was already being judged. I had already given up something that I could never get back and I could not have another chance to do it over. Once you make that decision it is final. I felt like I was stuck with him and what other guy is going to want to be with some girl that just gives herself away so easily? I felt like nothing. So, because I felt like nothing, I put up with everything. Eventually, Xavier got tired of just getting away with everything that he was doing, and he broke up with me to be with another girl. I was devastated. I thought that I had finally fit in. I thought that I had finally belonged. I thought this was everything that I was waiting for in my life. I thought that because I was with Xavier, and he was popular this meant that I could never speak up for myself or be recognized by others. I thought that giving myself and my heart to him was everything that I needed to do to keep them. And I'm not saying that I gave myself to him to keep him I'm just saying that because I loved him. I thought that love was enough. It's so funny now looking back how even as an adult many people who search for themselves and someone else. But being in a relationship does not make you feel whole if you are not already a whole individual it makes you feel lonely and points out your flaws.

A few weeks later Xavier came to school with a Hickey on his neck. This was another opportunity to leave. I asked him where it came from. He said that his foster sister came on to him and he pushed her from him. Again, I was angry, and I felt like less and less of a person the more I stayed with him, but for some reason, I could not leave. I started to feel like if I leave him and I only felt like I was enough with him then maybe I should say. Then there was the fact that so many other women wanted him it made me feel useless. So not only was I going to break up with him, but I would see it being thrown in my face every day. I started talking to other boys and flirting as well. It started to become a sick game who could hurt who first. I did not want to give myself to anyone else, but I wanted to get even. How could he hurt me when he said he loved me? I had never been in a relationship like ours before. I was not sure if every relationship was like this. I wondered if every girl or woman in a relationship as serious as ours had to deal with some type of disappointment. I started to think my standards are too high because of our position in a social setting, I thought popularity equated to quality. I was born to bear the burden of disappointment. In my heart, it felt wrong, but I did not think I could handle seeing him with someone else and rubbing it in my face. I did think that I loved him and at my youthful age, I felt like we would have been together forever. As if forever was not a long time. We continue to walk the halls together. He was not just an all-around bad guy. He did good things as well like the time he bought me a camera. We went on our first date to my favorite restaurant. When he got home, he told me that he got sick from the food at the restaurant. Slowly but surely the excuses started. He had an excuse for not calling me back. He had an excuse for rumors about other girls around school. He had an excuse for the girls that I heard in the background of our phone conversations.

    He made me feel like I was crazy. I kept thinking about how insecure and paranoid could I be. Was this all in my head or was he trying to play me the whole time?

It was something about him that made me stay with him. I was angry most of our relationship and I felt so disappointed in myself. I gave him a part of me that I could never get back and everyone in school knew it. They looked at me like I was a whore, and I felt a piece of me slip away. The next day Xavier broke up with me to be with someone else. Do you know how it feels to finally fit in just to be rejected again? Knowing that someone that I love felt like or thought that I was not good enough. I was so upset. I was devastated. I tore and cut up all our photos. I cried and cried until I was empty of tears. I was in a dark place. I felt like why I am even here. How can I be allowed to feel this much pain? It may not be right away, but one cannot escape the consequences of one's actions. It felt like God allowed me to be punished and Xavier got to walk away with not a care in the world. I kept imagining him laughing when he broke up with me playing repeatedly in my mind. I thought of him saying that I would never find anyone else like him ever again for the rest of my life. I thought of being in school together and seeing him with someone else the way that he used to be with me. A scream escaped me that sounded like the tragic loss of someone at a funeral. I did not want to be here anymore. I just wanted the pain to stop. It was not a physical injury that you can see the blood and the scab and then throughout the time you could see it start to heal. This was the type of pain that felt like it would never go away. I picked up the closest thing to me on the floor as my body lay exhausted on the bed and ran into the bathroom where I did something I thought I never would do.

  I lay, there on the cold bathroom floor thinking that it would be over soon but thank God that the cut was not deep enough. I put a cloth around my arm, and I had this feeling that I needed to take the thought of dying out of my mind and getting some rest. I woke up late that night while my television was still playing and the song by Mary J Blige called "Be without you" was on and it was on the part where they got back together, and I felt peace. I opened and closed my eyes once more then drifted to sleep. That night I dreamt that I was somewhere sometime in the future. I was living in a house with white columns and inside the house was sitting in a chair holding a baby girl that looked like Xavier. I had this weird sense that we will be back together, but I felt like I was only getting a part of the story. The next day a few of my friends and some guys were nice to me. They said that he was crazy to let me go. It made me feel better, but I was so immature that I did not allow my heart and soul the time that it needed to heal. I was in a new relationship by the next week and another and another looking for someone to heal my pain. I hurt every guy that I was with because I was so afraid of getting hurt again. It is true what they say hurt people hurt people. What I should have done was take the time I needed to reflect on a relationship and know that just because he hurt me did not mean that I should hurt other people who did not deserve it and even if you make the mistake of giving away your body it does not and I repeat it does not mean that your body is not still a temple and that you should not be cherished and respected. You should be respected and cherished. I wish

I had waited for the husband that God made for me instead of my first real relationship. I should have focused on my education and myself so that I could have become the woman I was always destined to be. We are so much more than our bodies. Take care of your body, your health, your mind, and your heart because honestly you and God are the only ones looking out for you. When you respect yourself, others will follow your lead. Sex is not as important as someone who speaks to your soul because it is so much more than someone who only gives to your body. So be good to yourself.

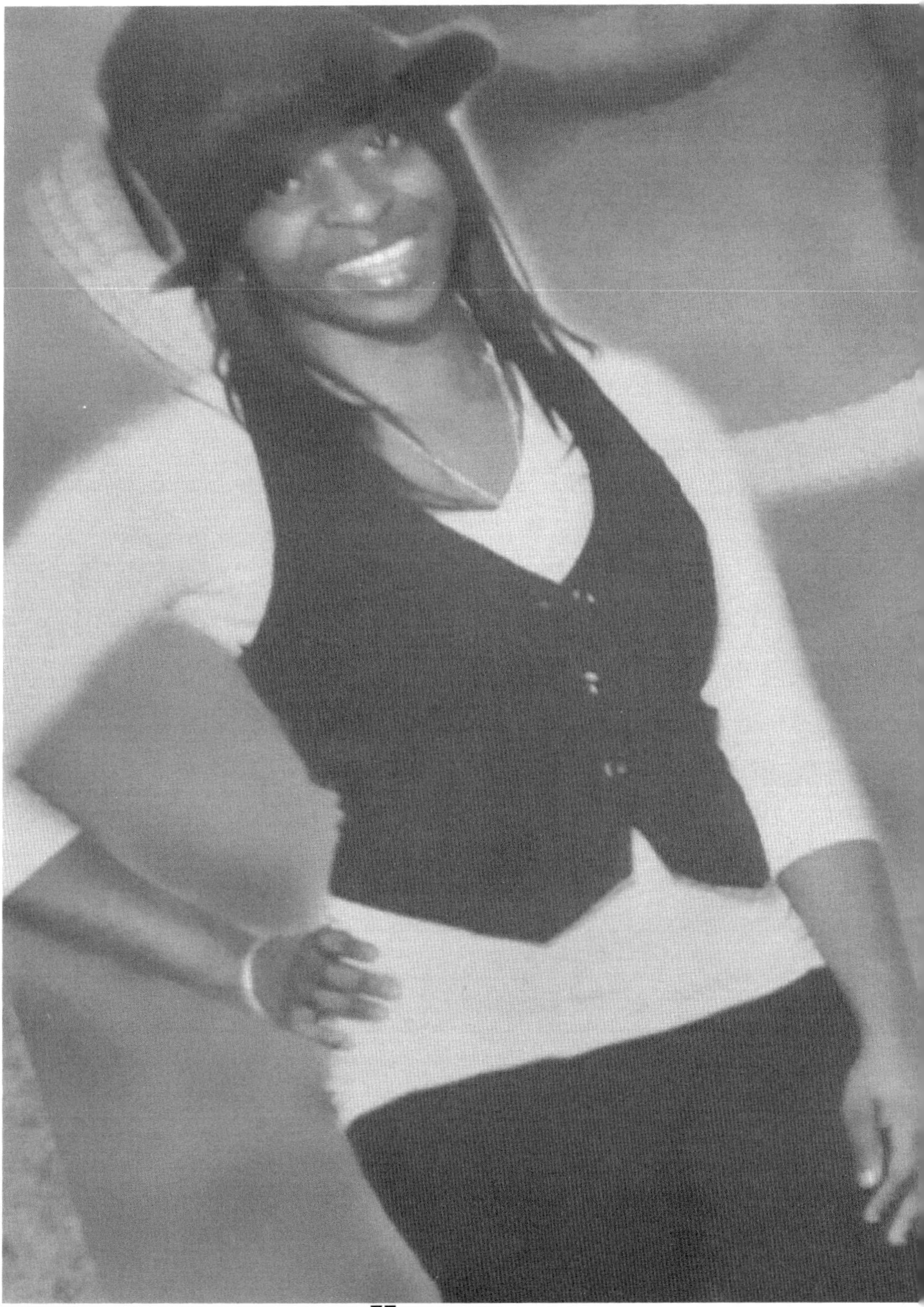

"David's father did not see the purpose."

Acts 13:22

Chapter 6
Tragic Comfort

I do not know what drew me back to Xavier, but it was like something kept pulling us together. When Xavier and I reconnected, we were both so young and so lost.

We had no idea how to love or what real love was. I knew after some time had passed; that I never felt the way I did about Xavier with anyone else. Xavier was so smooth he barely had to break a sweat to catch your attention. He put you in a trance and seduced your mind. The words he spoke were like poetry and they caught your heart in your mind like a fish in a net. Xavier was one of the most handsome men I had ever met in my life but soon I would learn a relationship life partner was more than appearance. I wanted no I needed to prove to myself that I could be with someone and keep someone like him. I let him get away with trivial things that did not seem to be that big of a deal like smoking and lies that were right on the borderline of a deal-breaker. He had a way of talking his way out of anything. He would say he was trying but most of the time I felt like I was in a relationship with a ghost. When I was 21, we moved in together. Even though we lived together I could see him, but he was not present. He would sleep most of the day, smoke, or work. When he was home, he did not want to do anything together. He would let me have my way when we had a disagreement and then guilt me into feeling bad about any decisions I made or standards I would try to make. I would have to keep telling him the five things I did not like repeatedly every day. Every day I felt so drained and exhausted. I felt like he was sucking the life out of my soul. My dream guy turned out to be a nightmare. I spend so much time worrying about his looks that I did not even consider looking at his character. His looks were a 20 on a scale of 1 to 10 and his character was a two when he decided to give minimal effort.

I should have been with someone on my level, not someone who was at a different level in the first place. There was a guy who liked me and treated me well that I was friends with. He was very handsome, and he had the same mindset as I did. He was the type of person I should have given the respect and attention that I gave to Xavier. When I was younger, I spent so much time focusing on all the wrong things and all the wrong people. I focused on all the wrong people instead of appreciating all the people in my life that loved me. I gave so much attention to a guy who would not care if I were in an accident on the side of the road and he spotted me gasping for breath. I needed to do better. I needed to appreciate everyone in my life who genuinely loved me, and I hope you will do the same.

"For God so loved the world, that He gave His only begotten Son, that whosoever believeth in Him should not perish, but have everlasting life." John 3:16

Chapter 7
Codependency

I do not know what drew us together but the pull that he had on me was unlike anything I had ever known. When Xavier would look at me my heart would race, and my stomach would feel like it was doing flips.

When he entered the room everyone else disappeared. I do not think there was ever a time that we communicated well. Every insecurity we felt we pushed on each other. It was as if I got this man but never got a chance to enjoy him. That is why people say be careful what you wish for.

I would like to pretend that the relationship was all bad, but I can honestly say that there were some good times like going to the movies, watching television shows together, going on a walk in the neighborhood, staycations, mini-vacations, dancing in the living room, listening to what we would like to have called old music, telling stories about our past, or even just riding in the car together... but every good day was overshadowed by something bad. When we would go to the movies most of the time it was something he wanted to watch. I learned that lesson quickly. If I even thought of picking something that brought me joy, he would be in a bad mood the entire night. He would either fall asleep during the movie or after the movie he would be so quiet that you could hear and feel the distance between us.

How could I expect someone to want to be with me when I at the time did not even want to be with myself?

I always felt on edge and like I was missing something. I felt like he hated me. I felt like I was with a stranger, but I was with someone who had always been that way I was just so stuck in his eyes, his perfect skin, his smile, and the way he spoke that put you in some sort of spell. His words made me feel like he was only talking to me and when he spoke it could uplift me or break me. He was so strong it made me feel invisible and weak. I wanted him to see me for me, to love me the way that I was, but how could he love me when I never gave him the chance?

I was so willing to just be with him with little effort, with little self-acknowledgment, with little devotion, with little loyalty, with little hope, with little honesty, with little joy, with little peace, and more importantly with little to no LOVE.

Where was the love? Did I ever love him? Did he ever love me? Was I just a piece of a whole person just searching for something to piece me back together? What was I going back to when I never really knew who I was? I was looking for him to fix me, to love me in a way that I had never loved myself. It is hard to get love from someone when you do not love yourself or have a relationship with God. I wanted him to be everything to me, but God was my everything. He is a jealous God that places no man before him. I was in such a trance I could not even tell you when it began. He was able to get that kind of a hold on me because my body that I should have only been saving for my husband was given to him even before either of us even thought of saying the words I do. If we would have taken the time, we should have gotten to know each other perhaps things could have been different. I was over the relationship and ready to move on.

"God is the great I AM."
Joshua 1:9

Chapter 8
Losing Myself

After Xavier left the scene, I started dating other people. I became a serial dater. It was not that I wanted to be in a different relationship it is just that I finally felt accepted by someone again.

I thought that being in a relationship would give me some sort of validation. It did not. Being in a relationship made me feel like I wanted to hurt all those guys the way that Xavier had hurt me. I had been so heartbroken over Xavier that I felt like all guys were like this. How would I know any different? This was my first serious relationship, and it was one of the worst relationships that you could put yourself in. Eventually I ended up dating this guy named Mickey. Mickey was the type of guy that parents wish their daughters would date. He was handsome, he is tall, he was kind, he was patient, he was understanding, and he never ever pressured me to do anything at all. He took the time to get to know me. He even asked permission to date me. We hung out, but he always respected the time and made sure that he did not keep me on the phone late. He was the type of person who was so respectful to me. Mickey listened to me when I spoke and was a young man of his word. One day I was talking to him about how much I loved to skate and that it was one of the happiest moments of my life. I talked about winning the limbo and being able to go on the weekends with my friends and family. He noticed how happy it made me and on our 1st date he took me skating. Being with Mickey made me feel so peaceful. I did not have to do anything but just be myself. He was so nice to me that when he treated me well because of how badly Xavier was to me it made me feel like I did not deserve it. We dated on and off for a while mostly because of me not feeling good enough. Eventually, I flirted with another guy Rye who was also extremely popular. He was not a bad guy, but he definitely was not anything like Mickey. He had amazing eyes he was the complexion of caramel, and he was one of the best basketball players. Any girl in the school would have probably done anything to be with this guy. He did not really have to say anything to girls like he was not the type of guy that just had a bunch of game he just could look at you and smile and you would know okay wow he wants to be with me. He was a man of few words but every word that he said had weight. I do not know what it was that made me want to flirt with this guy maybe it was because of all the attention he had from everyone else or maybe it was because of his swag. I do not know what it was that drew me to this guy, but I had a perfectly good guy that I was with. I tanked the relationship on purpose. Mickey never did anything wrong I just felt insecure and undeserving of someone who actually treated me right especially after the way that Xavier had treated me. When Xavier had broken up with me, he told me that I would never find anyone else to be with me. He said that I will always be alone and that no one else would ever like me ever again for the rest of my life. I did not think that was important to me then, but I carried that conversation in every relationship that I was in after that. When Mickey found out that I flirted with rye he broke up with me as he should. I was sad but I just expected every guy to leave and to not really want to be with me. I always felt that I was not good enough. I thought there was something in me that made me undeserving of someone who would actually respect me. Now that I am older, I know that I intentionally ruined the relationship because I felt insecure because of that previous relationship, but as a kid I did not connect the dots. I thought every guy was going to be as mean to me as Xavier was. I thought every guy would treat me as badly as Xavier did. It took me until I became an adult to actually realize that not every person is the same.

  Eventually, in high school I started to join different clubs. At first, I joined choir. Choir was a lot of fun I started to find groups of people that I wanted to hang out with. The next activity that I joined was volleyball and the track team. I wanted to belong somewhere, but I just did not know where or how to house that energy that I wanted. I also never believed in myself after that. After being picked on, insulted, bullied, and treated badly in a relationship I felt like I had nothing left to give to the world. I thought that those two bad instances determined the whole trajectory of my life. When I was in the sports or the clubs, I would try but there was always something that stopped me. When I was in track I ran track, but I let my grades drop. To stay on the track team, you had to have at least a C in all of your classes and in one of my classes I was falling so far behind. My mom came up to the school and I talked to my AP English teacher about extra credit and other activities that I could do to add extra points to my grade or to make up some of the work that I had done and received a portrait on. She allowed me to re-write one paper and do one extra credit activity. Doing the extra credit allowed me to get my grade up but I was already off of the track team. It seemed like every time I was starting to belong somewhere the activity was taken away from me. This time it was nothing but my fault. It was like I could not focus. Deep down inside I would tell myself you can do it, but I kept on feeling all of these negative thoughts negating every positive thing that I was trying to tell myself. I would say things like you could do it and then my next thought would be why would I even try when I obviously cannot keep a boyfriend and I cannot succeed in sports, my grades are horrible, and I am not smart. But I was smart I just did not know that I was.

It was prom time in my senior year, and it seemed like no one wanted to ask me to prom out of all the relationships that I was in the entire school year this was the only time that I was not in a relationship. I had no one that had asked me to go. So, three weeks before prom I asked two of the guys from my church to go with me to prom. They were twins. Two days before prom I found out that this really attractive guy named Matt wanted to go to prom with me, but I had already had my escorts. Matt was a really kindhearted person who was super gorgeous. When prom date came me, and my two closest friends were dressed to the nines. We all had our gorgeous dresses on, and we had our dates. My parents ended up getting us a white limousine. We were riding in style. We went to the destination and took pictures the two guys who escorted me were complete gentleman they open the door, and they asked if I needed anything to drink and we posed for pictures and we danced. While they were getting me a drink one of the guys from school named Johnny came up and asked if I would take a picture with him. Johnny was gorgeous as well. I did not just go to school with only gorgeous people it just so happened that those were the people that I was around. He had the most beautiful hair you could ever imagine. He was Indian and African American, and the girls went crazy over him. I was so surprised that he did not have a date. I agreed to take a picture with him. After prom we started to communicate on the phone. Johnny told me that he had always liked me, but he was too busy being a player to actually consider us being in a relationship before. I felt like it was too late because if he was really interested in me then he would have tried to be in a relationship with me before that day. We remain friends but never dated.

Eventually, it was high school graduation time the heat was crazy. We had our graduation outside at what we called the pit. The pit was a place where we housed all of our football games. We sat out and we listened to the valedictorian and a few other speeches and then as my name was called, I collected my diploma and walked across the stage. At the end of graduation, we all through our hats up but we printed our names inside of our hats so that we could remember whose hat was who's. I talked to my family and my friends and asked them to come over for my graduation cookout. At my parents' house a few friends and I talked about keeping in touch. We had no idea how much things would change just after high school. Some of my friends had planned on going away to school some of us were staying behind and some of us had even started working a job. I wanted to go away to college, but I did not want my parents to have to pay all of that money just to go to a school. I wanted to be independent and pay for my own school I wanted to go to a local Community College so that I can pay as I go to school. My dad and mom still agreed to help with school. It seemed like I was on the right track, but I had trouble finding my purpose. I knew I wanted to help people and I thought I wanted to become a psychologist. As I started my first semester of college, I took on a few classes. I was staying focused and doing everything that I was supposed to be doing. Out of nowhere one day Xavier sent me a message on Myspace. Myspace is the equivalent of with Facebook is to you today. He would send me messages saying how much he regretted losing me. He would say he did not mean all the things that he said and if we got back together things would be different, he talked about how much he missed being around me, he said that I was the only girl that he was ever in love with, he said that he regretted all the decisions that he made in our relationship, and that he should have never broken up with me. This went on for about a month. Eventually, at the end of the month, he asked me if I would ever consider giving him another chance and that he really wanted to know what my decision would be because he really wanted to be with me. I told Xavier that I would go on one date with him. At this time, I had started dating this guy named Anthony. Anthony was a nice guy who was very handsome and dark-skinned. I have met Anthony's parents and they were very respectable Christian people. We would hang out and play video games. He even came over to my parent's house. One day we had this conversation about his old friend hitting on him and how he did not want to judge his friend but as he told me the story it seemed like he had feelings for his friend. I did not want to be the person that stood in the way of him being who he really wanted to be. I wanted to give him the option to be true to himself. It was not for me to decide but I also felt like I could not stay with him. I decided to reply two Xavier and go on a date with him. I got ready for our date and was so excited to be able to be taken out on a date. Xavier said he had all these plans for our date and that we would end up going to go see a movie but instead of going to a movie we ended up going to a fast-food restaurant. I do not want to be the type of girl that complains about the place that I was taken instead of enjoying the moment of where we were because who is to say that he could have afforded something more than that and especially at 18 or 19 years old. And I decided not to judge him. As we sat there a disabled person came into the restaurant and both Xavier and his friend made fun of him. I was so embarrassed. I thought I would never talk to him again. When we got on the phone, I told him how I felt about the situation he said that his friend was the one that was laughing and that he did not laugh but I told him that him joining in and laughing at someone else's expense is just as bad as being the person who is doing the bullying or who is making fun of someone. He apologized and he agreed that he would try to do better. For the next three months Xavier and I were inseparable. We spent every single day together. Until…

Xavier ended up in jail for a hit-and-run. He was under the influence and ran into a substance that should have killed him, but he walked away without a scratch. He ended up being sentenced to 2 years for a 1st offense. A year before the incident we discussed my leaving if he ended up in jail or prison. I know high standards, but you live, and you learn. I tried to stay with him at first, but I had serious codependency issues and every day without him was torture. The short phone calls and weekly visits were cruel and unusual punishment. Eventually, I could not take it anymore and I broke up with him. After we broke up, I had no intention of giving Xavier another chance especially after he claimed that he cheated on me.

A month or so later I started seeing Xavier's friend Conner. Connor was mysterious, hood, handsome, strong, caring, and cool. He was the type of person that could be in a room full of people and still make you feel like the only person there. He was the type of person that I could not see myself seriously date, but the more time that I spent around him, it was hard not to like him.

Being around him made me feel like I could be myself with no judgment. He wasn't talking down to me or treating me like a burden. He was a real friend.

When it got close to Xavier's release date, he stated that he never cheated he just never wanted me to wait for him. I felt so guilty especially when we got back together. I felt like I did not deserve to be happy ever again for the rest of my life. I took Xavier back. Whenever Xavier would do something, I did not agree with I would speak up, but I would not stand my ground. After all, I felt like I had no right to verbalize how I truly felt because I needed to be punished until I died. I started doing more for Xavier than I did for myself. Friends would invite me to go places, but I would stay home. I felt like why I deserved to have fun or to even have friends with all the mistakes that I made in my life. That is especially since everyone in my life left eventually so why even try? I even changed my style. I started wearing clothing that felt more appropriate for someone in a relationship. I did not want to come off as easy or available to anyone. I wanted to look taken.

When we would go out or I would go to the store I would look down because I did not want Xavier to think that I was giving any attention to anyone else or that I was looking at anyone in a way that would make them think I was giving them the eye in any way or any woman to think I wanted to be with their significant other.

When birthdays or holidays would come, I would make sure I got Xavier something that he always wanted or mentioned in passing. I did this because I knew Xavier never got a real Christmas growing up like the one that I had all my life and that made me feel guilty as well. I would try on my job but not too much because I was afraid of being more successful than Xavier. I still managed to get a promotion at every job and every time I got a promotion Xavier looked at me with hate and disgust. He would always make me feel so guilty. I started taking classes to finish a degree and stayed focused. Every year he would have an excuse of why he hated his job, and no one would give him a chance and continue to job hop. I felt so much pressure on my shoulders, but I was too afraid to ask for help because why should I when I was getting what I deserved. Eventually, Xavier's family came to visit, and they would walk all over me, and Xavier would let them. I did not want to disrespect his family, but I felt so stressed out. I talked to Xavier about it, and he blew me off as if I had no right to tell him I was not okay with anything his family did. He continued to invite them over and I felt myself shrink. I became angrier and more resentful.

  The relationship became more toxic because Xavier was always job hopping. I took on odd-end jobs while I took classes. One day his family said they were coming down and showed up unexpectedly and I had just worked a strenuous job. I had a lot of cramping back pain and headaches. When I got home, they arrived shortly after. I felt nauseous and horrible I went to the bathroom and felt like I was having mini contractions. I could hear Xavier laughing and talking with his family. He did not even check on me. I investigated the toilet and there was blood and there was something that looked like a small embryo on that issue as it was under me. My heart stopped I did not know I was pregnant because I was on birth control. I was in shock. I stayed there for about half an hour. I did not want to tell Xavier because I was worried, that he would blame me or worse not care at all. I placed the embryo into the toilet and flushed it down the drain. It was a little smaller than a pea and I felt horrible. My headache was so bad. I looked at Xavier as I headed to the bedroom. His sister checked on me to see if I was okay. I told her I had a bad headache. I took some Advil and tried taking a nap. I cried alone in the dark that night. I was confused as to why I was sad when I knew I did not want another child with Xavier. I always said horrible things about only wanting the one child that we had and felt guilty like this was my fault. The next day I told Xavier and all he said was oh. He showed no empathy at all. We talked about it as time went on and about trying to have another child. We tried for three years but were unable to have another child and I felt so guilty. Not only had I dated his friend after we broke up but now, I could not have his child. As time went on, I felt myself vanish. It was all about Xavier and I felt so much anger and sadness toward him. I felt invisible.

On my 30th birthday in November, I broke up with Xavier. I told him how I had been feeling neglected and miserable. He said he was miserable as well and we agreed to break up. When we broke up, I felt like my world was gone. I did not know who I was anymore. I had stopped designing my nails because Xavier hated it when I did them because of the smell. There was not anything that I did for myself in years, and the saddest part is that I did not even notice. I felt like there was nothing left. I knew something was wrong if I felt this horrible over a breakup. I was literally on the ground in the fetal position. Xavier said that he wanted to work it out and we had agreed to go to counseling. My mom set up a hair appointment for me to get my hair straightened in December. I felt a boost in my self-esteem that I did not even know that I needed. This was the start of my self-care journey. I needed to figure out who I was, and it was making me see our relationship from a whole other point of view. A week later my dad gave me, my mom, my brother, and his fiancé a mini trip to Williamsburg to stay a few days and go shopping. I brought things I never imagined getting for myself. I felt like someone does care about me and the people who love me do see me. They really see me. It made me feel like I do deserve better. I started dating myself and I became increasingly confident, and I could see Xavier look at me like he hated me for it. I started setting standards and learning better ways to communicate. We were not getting better at communicating and I could tell that Xavier did not like it. Xavier would say things he knew I would not like. He would make fun of me and hurt my feelings when I told him to stop, and he told me I was being too sensitive. I started to get fed up.

    Looking back, I realize that my relationship with Xavier had been bad ever since the moment I gave myself to him. He was my first real relationship. Before I gave myself to him, I considered myself strong. I judged other women who put up with the nonsense that I endured. Before I gave him all of me. He was kind, attentive, loving, caring, and charismatic. He seemed as if he would do anything for me. I kept thinking back to why I stayed with him after he started to change. Part of me was so embarrassed that I gave away something that I could never get back to. Someone that did not deserve it, no matter what I thought. I thought I was insecure before that. But after that, I became angry, obsessive, jealous, doubtful, and insecure. I felt like I was going crazy. He had me believing I was crazy. I felt like a joke to him. I wish I would have waited until I was married and found someone who loved me for my mind before he wanted my body. I was so much more than that. Therefore, I think that it is so important to know who you are. Know your worth and wait. Each time you have sex before marriage, you become increasingly insecure especially if that is not the person God intended for your life. I was so hard on myself when I did not need to be. I kept thinking, who waits until marriage anyway? A profoundly good man is not real. A real man does not exist. If only I would have focused on school and stacking my account by focusing on my future and who I wanted to be and not whom others expected me to be. You see, I always felt different and ashamed for not always fitting in. I used every opportunity to be like everyone else when I should have been true to myself. I spent so much time on bad men and worldly lust that I destroyed my chances of meeting a healthy partner. If I would have known all I had to do was ask for God's forgiveness. Do better. Set standards. And stick to it to be genuinely happy, I would have done that from the beginning. All the confusion I had in my life was because of myself and the devil. Remember, if you are in any situation where your intuition feels uneasy and are confused in that relationship the relationship is probably not for you. If you are in any situation dealing with a relationship, you will not be confused in that relationship. If the relationship is healthy. Your heart and mind will not be at war with each other. As Tony Gaskins Jr, says, "God is not the author of confusion." Anything of God will bring you peace in your heart and your soul. I am not saying that there will not be difficulties but there will not be physical fights and destruction of your self-esteem. You will feel special because you are special. You will feel full of love and peace. And not sadness, anger, and insecurity. The person you are with will look at you with so much love. You will feel it in your soul, and they will not let anyone put you down because that would be destroying a piece of them. These are just a few things. The difference between me from then to now is that I love myself and I do not want any relationship. I mean absolutely nothing in my life that is not of God. The piece that I have is something I will not change for anyone, not even my family. God wants us to have it all, and I give myself to him completely. He is everything to me. No relationship in my life has ever made me feel the way that God has. The amount of certainty, peace, love, acceptance, and security that I feel is not like anything I could have imagined.

I was so used to drama and feeling insecure. I thought something was wrong. I wish I would have known I could have felt like this from the beginning. If I had known that I would have done it God's way first and forever.

"*God presented Christ as a sacrifice of atonement, through the shedding of his blood to be received by faith."*

Romans 3:25

Chapter 9
Finding My Purpose

The more I started to learn, the more I began to find my purpose. I started taking Self-Love courses about the healing period after a breakup. I started to do the things that I used to do that I loved.

I started to think about what I love to do that brought me joy like fashion, writing, crafting, dancing, and dinner. I started doing one thing every month that I was afraid to do or things that made me uncomfortable. That was good for me. I started to date myself. I know it sounds crazy. It was a crazy idea for me, but I needed to learn who I was from the beginning. In my mind, I thought I would feel lonely and embarrassed eating out or doing things by myself, but honestly, no one cared that I was on a date alone. On my first date, I did my makeup, and my hair booked an appointment, and went to dinner at my favorite restaurant. Usually, I reserve this for my birthday every year, but this time I wanted to go and enjoy myself. In the past, I would want to go out with Xavier, and Xavier would make me feel so guilty about wanting to go out or he would be so disconnected from our date. I would feel angry and sad because I was the one that wanted to go out. I do not know why I felt like I had to wait for Xavier or my friends to be available to go out to dinner, the movies, the mall, the park, the museum, etc. I soon realized that I only needed myself to do those things. I was responsible for my happiness. I do not know why it took me so long to reach that realization, but once I found it, I knew there was no turning back. I created a crafting business that is dedicated to helping others believe in themselves. I know I would not have done that if I did not start to believe in myself. I could feel myself gaining more confidence. I started to think of what I wanted to wear or what I wanted to do that made me happy and not what I wanted to do because I constantly was seeking approval from others. When I would get dressed previously, I wanted to dress for Xavier and my family. I wanted them to feel comfortable around me. I was so afraid of being perceived as loose or looking like a loser that when I thought I was trying I was so in my head. I felt uncomfortable in every outfit. I felt like why try to please others when I knew there was no way I could please everyone. I felt so uncomfortable in my skin as if I were someone else, and technically I was not being myself. I did not know who I was. I knew I wanted to be successful and take care of myself. But before the process, I never took the time to see what I like and truly find out who I was. I would keep toxic people in my life or trade one toxic person for another and think this is just life. This is not just life. I deserve better and more. And everyone else does too. If you lead in love, stand up for yourself, and remove toxic people from your life you can truly be happy. Happiness is a state of mind and honestly believe me when I say that your mind is the most powerful tool in your body. Your most powerful tool is not your hips, your buttocks, and your lips. It is your mind. My mind helped me believe in myself and I can feel the peace from the knowledge that I obtained from courses, counseling, and other things that helped to improve my health, body, and skin. I have always been beautiful, but as soon as I started working on myself, I could see that now. I now feel beautiful in the way that I treat others, I take accountability for any actions that I make and set standards for how I allow others to treat me. When I do this, I come from a kind and loving place, and those who genuinely care about me understand. I try not to hold on to others' emotions because I know that it is their journey to bear, and I can only control how I react to any scenario in my life and how not how others perceive the message. I do not go out of my way to hurt anyone, and now I know that does not make me weak because I have standards, and once I tell someone how they make me feel. I hope that they respect me. I also try not to be too sensitive if something is not an actual joke. I have had friends tell me hard truths and I accept it because it is coming from a good place. We also try to uplift each other and now that we are honest with each other, I have noticed our relationship grow and we have become closer. It also allowed me to have a healthy outlet so that I am not letting my emotions build up and explode somewhere else. Not every day is a walk in the park, but there is something about knowing who I am that makes me feel like any sadness I feel will not last always. Every day when I wake up, I think of one thing I am grateful for, and I thank God. They say that "faith without works is dead" James 2:17. What does that mean? At first, I thought that meant working at a job or relationship, and yes, it can be that as well. Now in my process of growing in my religion growing in my faith and my personal growth in my outer and inner self I have learned that the work that is mentioned means so much more than just an effort put forth in one area or another. Work means working on everything from my stank attitude to my appearance, to my faith, to my job, to my business, to my confidence, to my mind, and serving. It means learning to stand for something that truly matters and listening to God and my intuition. It means being the person God intended me to be through whatever circumstance and scenario I need to grow and learn from. In the past when dreadful things would happen, I would feel like this is as low as it gets. I would feel like this is all my life is. I figured someone had to be miserable so why not me. This was a good question. Just as easily as it was to place blame, look at the dark side, and feel down on myself. There was just as much Good. That could have convinced me to turn the other cheek, look within, look at the bright side, and think why not me. I need to be the inspiration I need in my life and not the sadness I knew before I started my journey. Why could I not forgive and forget so that I could take that lesson and learn from it? Why could I not look within myself to be better and use every lesson as a steppingstone to be better? With each step forward it moved me to a higher level and a better version of myself. I started thinking it could be me and it can be you too.

There is so much hate and negativity in the world. We need to even the score. We need to step up because someone must. I want the world to be better for my daughter, for my family, and for generations to come. I want every person to have somewhere to turn, no matter where they are in life. I want to change everything from the sinners to the whores, to the heartbreakers, to the last, to the confused looking for guidance for the work in progress, and for the people who are looking to grow. I want to make sure no other child, woman, or relationship needs to endure the things that I have endured with the help of this book and others like mine.

Let us change the world!

"Moses and Aaron went in and told Pharoah, Thus saith the Lord God of Israel, let my people go." Exodus 5:1

Chapter 10
Becoming Independent

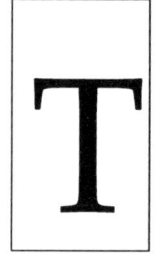

To me when I first gained my independence, I thought this is it I have arrived at my destination. Boy was I wrong. I felt on top of the world for the first few weeks. I thought sadness was behind me, but it was not. There would be good and bad days. The sadness that I felt on this day consumed me. It felt like a heavy weighted blanket over my mind, body, and soul. I listened to my daily motivation, but I was stuck. I felt all these negative emotions like why try when no one cares anyway, God says that I am here to inspire others and at that moment I could not see that. I felt like my purpose was gone. The inspiration that I felt every day before felt like it was pulling itself away from me. I felt so uncertain. I could not understand where all this doubt was coming from. My heart felt heavy. I kept questioning everything in my life. Was I right to leave Xavier? I just started having flashes of him not wanting to spend time with me and putting me down but saying it was a joke. The insecurity that I felt when I was with him, sleeping alone when he would always go out in the middle of the night to get high. I had to keep reiterating my needs, but when he wanted or needed something I always felt like I did not have a choice. The stress of worrying about him quitting a job and feeling the stress from the family that he worked with when he chose to call out the morning that he worked. The constant job change made me feel like a horrible person because I did not want his family to live with us or smoke drugs at our home because of our daughter and my job. My standards were unimportant to him.

  The more things I started to do that I like, the more I felt myself become more confident and in turn, I became more independent. I started wearing outfits that I love no matter what anyone else thought about them. I would not wear anything overly sexual, but I looked nice, neat, and put together without being stuffy. If I liked my outfit, that was all that mattered to me. I started using new cream for acne scars. I take care of the strawberries on my legs by moisturizing and having better shaving habits. Even when my nails were not done, I kept them neat and clean. I made a schedule for myself for pedicures and alternated every two weeks with home pedicures that my daughter and I did as a girl's day. I go on me-dates once a month to remind myself to love myself. I started using better moisturizer for my face, and my skin that I applied with care every day. I started taking more time with my hair and made sure to keep my hair nice, neat, and organized. I used to just throw it in a ball and go. I took my time making sure I had a wash day schedule and I stuck to it. I made it fun by picking new styles for my hair that would keep my hair healthy and would not constantly need to be changed. I would stick with one style every week. Now, when I do put my hair in a bun, I take the time to make sure that I pay extra close attention to the ends of my hair, so that I can make sure it stays moisturized. When it comes to brushing my teeth, I switched from a manual toothbrush to electric and water flossing instead of regular flossing that would hurt my gums. I made sure that my eyebrows are neat. I found perfumes that I liked and looked up techniques that allow body sprays to last for a long period. I not only took the time to work on my outward appearance, but I also worked on the inside. I continued going to counseling. I took courses to learn more about business. I started listening to a podcast about emotional intelligence. I took courses on trades that I always wanted to learn. I started reading more books and the Bible. I listened to financial podcasts that helped build a business from the ground up. I listened to more sermons from different pastors online. I started attending Bible study every Wednesday and church every Sunday. I started being mindful of the things that I said. I started acknowledging my wrongdoings and apologizing for them. Even if I was hurt or angry, I realize I can only control how I reacted, and it made me feel better on the inside. Before I knew it, the only thing I would have relied on is God. I appreciate the people in my life that have always been there for me and those who may be harsh or blunt but are coming from a good place. My heart feels so light now. I used to feel like I had this heaviness over my body and my soul, and now I started to feel like I am enough for myself because I am a child of God, I have nothing else to prove to anyone else. Occasionally, I get a negative thought about being alone or not being worthy. But I know that is just a horrible thought and nowhere near the truth. Every negative thought I have, I counter it with two positive thoughts, and I say a quick prayer. All these things start leading me in the right direction.

    Do you know that old saying? If you do not stand for something, you will fall for anything. Well, that is so true even when you think you are being tough, or you are saying something. When I was younger and in my relationship with Xavier, I always felt like I was standing up for myself. But raising your voice does not mean that you are standing up for yourself. I thought an argument was normal, but it was not. You do not need to raise your voice or put your hands on someone that you are supposed to love, or someone that you claim to love. That is not real love. Real love is patient, kind, and it is understanding.

"Whoso finds a wife finds a good thing and obtains favor of the Lord." Proverbs 18:22

Chapter 11
Gaining My Independence

I left Xavier. I learned who I want to become and there were some things I no longer accepted. I had standards and non-negotiables.

Before, I thought the only thing I deserved was sorrow. I thought I needed to be punished for any wrong decision I had ever made. I was so hard on myself. I was feeling sorrow, anger, and disappointed at times when I should have appreciated every moment I was allowed in life. I had people in my life who loved me through it all. I had family and friends who accepted me as I was, even when I could not see myself being any better than a disappointment. God believed in me even when I did not believe in myself, and that is why I am eternally grateful to him. He saw me as the person he created, even when I accepted being treated like a second choice. Even when I allowed people in my life that made me feel worthless, he protected me from people I allowed in my life, but he knew better. He allowed people to enter my life. That changed my mind set and made me believe in myself, even in times when I felt weak or like I could never move on. I thought I needed to be with someone. I told myself I did not need a man but deep down I felt desperate for that feeling of being wanted and accepted. God already accepted me. He accepted me through being hardheaded. Low self-esteem, bad attitude, and even when I was lost. I thought my life was more like that. I determined what happened in my life, but he proved to me he was in control. Every choice I made led me to this moment in my life. When I think back about things that I wish I had done differently I realize it had to happen because of the choices I made. At first, I felt guilty because when we broke up, and then I felt peace and joy. I was sad for a few days because of the time, and I know things would change. But by day three, I thought things will change. I started to think of all the things that I always wanted to do. My ex would say things like it were hard for him and I would feel guilty that it was not hard for me. I felt like everything was going to be okay. I know a relationship takes two people and I take responsibility for the parts that I played in our demise, but I needed to move on. He did not want me. He did not treat me like anything but an after I thought. He did not cherish me or our time together, and I needed to be with someone who loved me. The way that I was beginning to love myself.

There is no other way I could have just believed in myself or witnessed my miracle. I was so weak, and I do not know how else I could explain the strength that I felt right now. Anything was possible and "I could do all things through Christ who strengthens me."

It is so funny that every time I have control over my life the Lord humbles me quickly. For example, one day I filled out for a position with exemplary pay, and I all but felt like I had the job in the bag. You know what happened is that I got no call back the position was closed the people were exhausted or the numbers did not match up. When God is in your job, your career, your relationship, and your school selection it is smooth sailing, and everything lines up. I have qualified in the past for jobs that I was underqualified for, and I know that it was nothing but God, who gave me that position. I have qualified for jobs before that all but disappeared and that was nothing but God as well. So many times, I wondered why the relationship did not work out and the person ended up in prison for murder or rape and all that I could do was thank God. Sometimes I felt like God was just trying to make things harder on me when he was building me and humbling me so that I could be used in the way he needed me to be used and I could be a humble servant instead of a proud disobedient know at all. I thank God for that. God allowed me to be humble in his work is the best gift he has ever given me. I want to help people. How can I help someone if I was walking around like I was better than everyone else? I could not help anyone. I would be more hurtful than helpful. God has taught me so much that I need to learn in my humbling season. I am not patient, but I have learned to be more patient. I am not the type of person who believes in slowing down and God reminds me to take in the time with family, with my friends, and every type of relationship or job when they may not be there one day for me to appreciate the time and the lessons that I would have learned by taking it all in. I am so thankful for his promise. He has kept me when I felt so lost, when I felt so sure, and even when I knew he was there with me. He was constantly there reassuring me every step of the way.

It is so weird now looking back because I always believed that through this entire process of gaining my independence, I was the only person experiencing pain or hurt. It was not until I was 30 years old that I really started to self-reflect. I considered how my ex or my old friendships or other people in general felt.

I felt this push of reaching out to the person who was with Xavier. The day during the phone call was weird, and I did not see how I could get anything out of it but why did I need to get something out of it when God specifically asks me to do it. I felt nervous but full after the phone call. I felt warm like I could feel God's love all around me. It was a feeling I never experienced before. I could feel myself doing what God instructed. Doing as God asked me to was not always easy. Sometimes I felt like I just did not want to do it. Sometimes I felt weird. Sometimes I felt like I was so outside of my comfort zone but that was the point. If you ever feel too comfortable, you are doing it wrong. I was having an out-of-body experience. I had so much joy peace and happiness that I knew I made the right decision. That is the purpose of obeying God and not the devil. If this were a distraction from Satan, I would have felt confused angry alone, and insecure, but I did not feel any of those feelings. Making the phone call allowed me to forgive Xavier. I cannot blame Xavier for my personality, for not sticking to my standards, for my naivety, for me feeling out of place, or for the time I spent in a relationship with him because I chose to stay. I did not want to see him for who he was or to see the relationship for what it was. I cannot blame Xavier for all the tears that I cried that he was unaware of. I cannot blame Xavier for his family when that is something no one can choose. I cannot blame Xavier for having a child at an early age. I cannot blame Xavier for getting married young. I cannot blame Xavier for getting together at 15 years old. I cannot blame Xavier for not seeing me when I never saw who I truly was or who I could become. I cannot blame Xavier for the women when I never trusted myself to decipher when my intuition had been trying to tell me all along. I cannot blame Xavier for not doing something he never learned to do.

    I now look at my marriage and past relationships as a big life lesson. I would not be a better person without it. I would not have been able to learn who I truly am without learning what I will and will not accept. Being in any relationship has taught me what I do and do not want. Through God and learning more about selfcare self-love and relationships, I have now known the dos and don'ts of any relationship that I aspire to have. I now know that I deserve better and refuse to ever settle again. I am a diamond in the rough. I have shared my past traumas, mistakes, and missteps because it allowed God to use me so that I may help others around me and possibly the world. Only through Christ is this book possible. I am forever grateful and will continue to be not perfect but a blessing to others until the day that the breath leaves my body (my vessel), and my soul goes on to be with God.

The greatest mistake we make after any type of breakup is that we want to blame the other person because we are hurt and those around us want everything to be so black and white when most relationships live in the gray area. Most of the time no one person is only all good or only all bad. No person or relationship is perfect. People around you may tend to see the good in the person you are with or the friendship you are in, but they do not see the good or inconvenient times you experienced in the relationship. People around you most of the time depending on the person did not want to see you hurt. They want you to be happy, but they also do not want to see you make up with a person after the issue or those quirks that annoy you, but they do not have to live with you in your relationship which is why it is so important to tell the whole story if you must talk to someone and not just your side of the story. You need to use discernment. Set your standards and stick to them. I do not mean a standard of where you put the toilet paper, I mean something real that in your heart feels wrong or hurts your feelings something that if you do not correct it would lower your self-esteem and change who you are. You must be honest with yourself and determine if you can live with the mistake or choice of your partner or your friend you cannot say you can and throw it in your partner's face. It cannot be something that makes you feel invisible and unimportant. No matter how much you want that partner or that friend staying when you know in your heart that is something that you honestly cannot let go of is hurting you both. If it is keeping you from a true friendship or the real relationship you should have been in. If you are doing something, you know is wrong most of the time you will not gain anything good and pure from it. When you decide to put yourself in another person's shoes and think about how that makes them feel think about how the person is affected by your decision. Think about how your child will feel if you decide to end things over something trivial and if it is still the best or right decision for you. Leaving Xavier was something I had to do for myself and our child because I settled and did not always set appropriate standards. I did not want our daughter to think that was acceptable to settle. I did not want her to see our relationship and think that this is how they should be treated or what she should put up with. I would need her to see how it feels and what it looks like to love yourself and one day I hope to show my child what a happy healthy and whole relationship looks like. I want him or her in any relationship to feel beautiful, important, and wanted. I do not want them to ever feel insecure, unwanted, unhappy, misused, and unloved. My child deserves true happiness as do I and I am happy alone and will be happy in a healthy relationship one day.

    I would like to pretend that after God pulled me from the ground, I was completely healed from the hurt and never felt that way again. I need to keep it real and let you know that the struggle was not over, but my heart posture longed for reconciliation. I could not help but hope that Xavier would be completely changed and would have realize that I was the love of his life and see the pain that he had caused me. This is not to say that Xavier hurt me all on his own. I stuck around and allowed this man to hurt me. Not to say I was asking for it, but I let things slide that at the time I thought was a compromise for a better relationship. But looking back, in reality, I noticed that I was just looking like a weak woman who stood for nothing and fell for everything. I always assumed that a troubled relationship would be black or white, and it would be easy to decipher, but when you are in a troubled relationship, you start being oblivious to any game that is being played. I wanted to believe that he would not hurt me, especially since we were serious about the consideration of having a child, but little to my surprise I noticed that Xavier had little regard for me or a child. It was the Xavier Show day in and day out while I slowly disappeared. I could feel myself yelling and no one hear me. I was in a tunnel or a soundproof room or the middle of a lifetime movie calling for help, but no one could hear me scream and the sad part is that I let him let me disappear. I thought I had a voice, but he took that from me. He was so good. He would pretend as if he stopped making bad choices or started treating me better or listening to me, but he was not any better. I would express how I felt. He would pretend to listen and then do whatever he wanted with little to no regard for how I truly felt. He would say things like you always get what you want. We would have a discussion come to a compromise and then replay the same disagreement repeatedly. He would do this thing where he would pretend that he was letting me win, and then he would guilt trip me about it every day. Because of how far I have come. I know I am not going to allow me to be in any other relationship like that again.

The work on myself does not end. Spiritual warfare is real. There will be things that have happened, but they are not who I am.

"Know also that wisdom is like honey for you. If you find it there is hope for you."

Proverbs 24:14

Chapter 12

Independent

My relationship with Xavier was 15 years. At first, I kept trying to figure out why it was taking so long to heal. First off let me say there is no time limit on the healing process.

Take all the time you need and if you face your pain, you will eventually heal. I did a healing course from a relationship coach. In the course, Tony Gaskins Jr. talked about working on your 3 B's the Brain, Brand, and Body and it worked. I did not realize this at first, but I had just been working on myself and once I did the "Moving On" course, I learned what was holding me back and it was that I did not face my pain. I felt my pain the first three days but after that in my head, I felt like I should have been over it. I could not understand why I still felt stuck. I was doing my own thing and randomly a feeling of pain would hit me, and I would always brush it off and be so hard on myself. Now I know when I feel the pain I dig deep. I make sure all the things we had together were gone and make sure that we meet outside of the house if we must meet there or at any other location for exchanges of our child. I gave our daughter a photo of all of us and deleted the rest and honestly, I felt exhilarated. I felt like I was breaking one of the many chains that were tying me to him. I know I do not want us anymore. I would always think if only we had done this or maybe if we had done that it could have worked out but if we could have done this or that we would have been together. There is no chance that I want to be with the person he is, and I hated who I was when I was with him. Our daughter deserves the best of me and even though I do not feel absolutely anything towards our old relationship it does not mean I will not have the memories.

Another thing that helped me is telling whoever I talked to that I do not want to talk about Xavier. It helped me to have my ex removed from the conversation and keep the conversation on my relationship with my friends and family lives. It removes them from reentering your mind even in a conversation.

For me, it was the hardest because of our child but if you do not allow them to get to you emotionally, they do not have another way in. I was unintentionally leaving the door cracked for someone that I knew I did not want and then I was wondering why I could do all the work on myself counseling, exercising, working on my business, writing, listening to inspirational messages and gospel music, and affirmations and still feel my heart murmur from time to time. I felt crazy and I was so hard on myself. Do not be so hard on yourself. If you were trying you were already halfway to healed. The rest of the way is your continued work on your outward and inward self.

I do not always have good days. I knew it may seem like I have it all figured out, but no one has it all figured out. I am constantly growing to become a better person in one way or another period I continue to look forward even when there seems to be no end in sight. Sometimes I feel like I am in a tunnel with no finish line, but I remain focused, and my obedience brings me through. It helps me to grow in every way that God needed me to so I could take everything I need from every struggle. Sometimes when I go through my time of limbo, and I reminisce about the unwise decisions I have made I gain new knowledge and learn new things about myself and Xavier or past friendships. I learn things that I did wrong that I did not even notice at the moment. I noticed red flags that look different to me when I was in the relationship. It was like I had a feeling about a situation but at the moment, it did not seem like it was that big of a deal. Without my standards there is nothing and I mean absolutely nothing standing in the way of the bright red flags. Without my standards, the red flags look like a small piece of red string that I could not make out through the lens that I call my eyes. Now, these red strings look like bright red flags right in front of my eyes waving with flashing red, orange, and yellow lights. It is so weird how you can give so much of yourself to a relationship that all you can see is your hope for the person you are with. It is like I had rose-colored glasses on. The person I was with could have been mentally abusive, a smoker, womanizer with gingivitis, and 12 kids with twelve different wives and what I saw was a guy who wanted to do better. He said all the right things that I wanted to believe so badly. I always thought no one is that evil that they would intentionally want to hurt the mother of their child and would be jealous, envious, and have so much hate for her. I thought he would want to love me and treat me right so our child could experience how she should be treated. He would love me the way he wanted our daughter to be loved and he would speak to me the way he would want someone to speak to our child but just because I had the best intentions, I am nowhere near perfect but just because my intentions were good does not mean that his or the other person's intentions will be good. Always remember that.

At the beginning of my self-love journey, I thought the only thing that I had to do was forgive Xavier and forgive others, but I never imagined forgiving myself. I needed to look within and know the mistakes that I made, acknowledge them, learn from them, and remember them so that I could move forward. I had this weird feeling where I felt like I was stuck in a loop of guilt and sorrow. I kept blaming myself and thinking well maybe if I had done this then it would not have happened. Maybe if I were not so hopeful for Xavier, I could have saved our whole relationship. Maybe if I had done whatever he wanted. Maybe if I did not vent about him to others. Pause. This is a big warning never talk about your relationship to anyone else. A lot of the time we think about how good it feels to get it off our chest when someone does something to us to hurt our feelings or mistreats us but when you are ready to forgive your partner your family and friends never forget no matter how much time passes. Also, on the other note if your partner does not respect you when you say they are hurting your feelings it is time to move on. I know how hard it is. Heaven knows I know but you get out of the relationship when you feel unheard, unappreciated, and disrespected, or would you rather spend 10 years in a relationship that you are not genuinely happy in. If you are not getting what you need from your partner, feel insecure, resent your partner, and start to lose yourself. You cannot give anything to a relationship when you are empty.

I see so many people give up or they turn to drugs or alcohol. I turn to God, and that is the only thing that separates us. God's love is stronger than any drug I had ever heard of. There are still trials that I face, but a lot of the time when I am down or in a hard place, I can see greatness on the other side. That is solely because of God's grace. If you had asked me before I went through this journey in my life. If this were possible, I would say no. I always thought I believed in God, but this journey made me feel like I was a fraud before. I went to church occasionally. I went from acting crazy, aggressive, and angry before and after church to be the same no matter where I was. I thought being in a relationship made me complete and I looked like I had it all together. I was so overlooking and acting like I was something I was not. All I needed was to be more like God. God is not looking for perfection. You do not want to be so Christlike that you cannot help the people on earth. All God wants us to be is the best that we can be and listen to him. That does not mean I go out looking for trouble because I will be forgiven. Even God has limits. If I do something I know is wrong, that is my burden to bear. If I say something that offends someone or react the wrong way, I reach out to reconcile the situation, because God knows my heart is in the right place, even if it is not how it is perceived. It is coming from a place of love. I focus on love, kindness, and God's word. Any bad thoughts that I feel? I know is a distraction because the journey that I am on gives me a piece that I have never witnessed in my life, and I would not trade it for anything. I do not feel like I am lacking or without anything. I feel like I have everything that I need. Sometimes I think back and the memories of me and Xavier just keep replaying in my mind. I think was it all that bad or am I dreaming that we are not together? It was just some cruel joke to try to teach me a lesson, make me beg for him, make me helpless, make me feel like I need him, and then I realize no, this is real life. He is gone. I asked him to go. I made myself write down a list right before I decided it was over and times like this. I look back at that list and it reminds me of all the hurt that I went through. And for every good moment. Or memory. The four bad memories combat the good. They are overshadowing any doubt that I may have felt about second-guessing myself. Someone once said that your body tries to protect itself from pain. You get a bee sting and suddenly you are careful around bees. You get hurt by a friend and suddenly you are more careful around every new friend even years later, you want to believe things could not have been that bad. Weather at a job or around a person following a horrific experience through time, it starts to seem as if it was not that bad. That is exactly what I was doing. I kept feeling myself wanting to blame every problem, every disagreement, and every misunderstanding on myself. But just as I wanted to say Xavier was not all to blame because I was willing to stay in a toxic, dysfunctional relationship so was he. I can only express how I felt and how I felt was so unloved and so unaccepted. Always. It may have been unfair of me to put so much pressure on Xavier. To make me feel accepted and as if I belonged. Whingeingly on all those years that I felt left out and did not belong. But shouldn't I feel that with my partner at the very least? I should have felt loved, and wanted to be included, respected, and appreciated. Anyone in a relationship deserves the same. Please do not settle because you are not only doing a disservice to yourself, but you are holding the other person back from their true potential while they are standing around giving you the bare minimum. People, we are so much more than that. Do not stop growing, loving, learning, and being because someone you love, whether that be a partner, family member, or a friend, is lost or insecure. Someone who wants to make you feel that bad has the worst type of insecurity that any human being can have. It is time to grow up and not play the blame game. I cannot blame Xavier, but I acknowledge it takes two people to form a relationship. This book is not

written to bash Xavier, but to set a precursor for red flags. A lot of us are so oblivious to it. It is so easy to see the red flags in this story, or your friend's relationship. But when it comes to being in a relationship. I kid you not, but those red flags, to me, seem like a red flag just sitting in the background of a room in the dark. I could see a glimpse of it, but I could not make out what it is. I hope that you can learn from my missteps. So, just maybe, you can make a better decision than I did. You are loved. You are blessed and You deserve peace in your
life.

When I first came to my independence, I thought this was it. I was on top of the world for a few weeks. I thought sadness was behind me, but it was not. There would be good and bad days. The sadness that I was feeling this day consume me. It felt like a heavy blanket over my mind, body, and soul. I listened to motivation, but I felt stuck. I felt all these negative things like why try no one cares anyway, God says I am here to inspire others, and right now I cannot see that. I felt like my purpose was gone. The inspiration that I felt every day before felt like it was pulling away. I felt so uncertain. I could not understand where all this doubt was coming from. This made me think of Napoleon Hill's book called Outwitting the Devil. How the devil wants us to drift so that we will not live out the purpose we have and. The life that we are prepared to live. My heart felt heavy, period. I kept questioning everything in my life. Was I right about leaving my partner? I just started having flashes of him not wanting to spend time with me putting me down, but saying it was a joke. I did not want his family to live with us and do drugs at our home, because of my job and the standards that I had that seemed unimportant to him. Making me feel bad because the dogs were outside in their insulated home, but he made me feel I could have my dream house when we had carpet floors throughout the entire house and the dogs shed a lot of hair and felt guilty because every time he wanted to pretend to do something nice or something for me, he would always take it away and throw it in my face. I get it. I felt like I deserved it because I dated his friend after we broke up 10 years ago. And that is how. I felt, but I knew that I deserved better. I love myself now and I know if he could not respect me or treat me right, there was no way that I could go back. I know that I was not a great wife either. I was controlling because I felt like I did not have control at all. I was needy because my life revolved around him. I was miserable because I kept giving little effort and setting, selling for less and everything I did. If there was a job opening, I would not give 100% of myself. In. The resume or the interview because I felt worthless to him and every time, I achieved something he made me feel ashamed of doing better than him. I was not trying to be better than him, but with him, I knew I was not doing my best. There were times when I would dress up or do my makeup and he would either put me down or make fun of me or give me a compliment followed by an insult. I kept trying to make him spend time with me and his daughter and he would rather sleep, smoke, play the game, go to the store or be with his other family members. I would be available for him after work or on the weekend, and he would say things like why don't we just stay home? Or we already live together. We spend time together because we are in the same house. He would let other people that he knew walk all over me, and when I spoke up for myself, he made me feel bad like I was being crazy. Or as if they were more important than his daughter's well-being. He would cuss at and or call our daughter names saying he was joking and when I would correct them, he would say I have no sense of humor, or I would make. Every day I felt so alone, but I stayed faithful throughout our entire relationship. I do not know why it took me so long to leave, but he had this hold on me that I could not be released from. He was like a black hole with a magnetic pull that sucked the life out of me. My daughter and I would have dance parties when he was not home and when he would return, I could feel the light go out of the room and all the happiness was replaced by indifference, anger, and sadness. It felt like the good energy was being sucked out of the House. I do not know if this were all in my head, but anything I mentioned I did not like or needed help with, he would do just to rub it in and I would get angry. I know how I should have been a better, bigger person and not let it get to me. I let him pull me to his level our whole life together, and until I knew my words, I never even noticed it. If you ever feel like something is not right, someone disrespects you. You feel like you must disrespect them. Without proper communication, someone will not be available for you, does not respect you, blames you, brings up mistakes you made, and throws it in your face or does not treat you the way you should be treated it is time to move on. It will be hard, but you will be happy with your Peace of Mind. It will build your self-esteem back up. It will allow you to recognize who you are. It will help you set your standards and you will become independent.

As I continue through my journey every day, I learn a little bit more about myself. Every time I think I have it all figured out; I learn that God is not through yet. I always exercise. So, I thought relying on food or other things was not something important that I needed to worry about. Ever again. But when I had a moment of weakness and ate one piece of candy that was horrible for me and it spiraled into me eating one unfortunate thing a day for a week and then the next thing you know, I must add more sweetener to my oatmeal and tea because of all the added sugar I ate during the week and now my body craves more. That is just one small example of when I thought I had everything figured out and that was something I can handle on my own, but God has time for all our problems. There is no problem that we can face in life that God will ignore. If we call on him and ask for his strength, he will help us. I have had moments where I felt overwhelmed. At work, at home, and in life, and as soon as I start to feel any sign of being out of control and or overwhelmed, I asked Jesus for his help to guide me through to take the stress away from me, to send help. And you know what he does? He shows me other ways to handle my scenario. He allows for the pressure and stress that I feel to fade away, and he turns it into motivational fuel. He opens another position at work out of nowhere and allows for my group or my family to come together to relieve any burden that I felt. As soon as I feel the devil trying to distract me with any negative feelings or mean people, I do what God would have me do, being slow to take offense, but always ready for reconciliation. Now that does not mean being a doormat for your enemy. However, it does mean to keep your class and show them how it is done in the most Christian way. Love your neighbor, love your enemies, and love yourself. At first sometimes it may feel like it is hard to love your enemies when they are hurting you, but the hate that you do have is fueling them and drawing cyphering from you. You have so much good to give to the world and you cannot let one person stop the promise God has on your life. Loving your enemies can seem impossible if you are always picking apart yourself, or if you are like me. You might treat your neighbors better than you treat yourself. How could you, how could I expect to find real love? I mean that God loved me even before I knew what it truly meant to love myself. How could I expect any man, person, family member, or friend to show me the respect that I did not even show myself? Ladies, men we must be better. Our children, family, and friends need to see what real love looks like. Not love that stems from abuse. Not love that stems from misuse. Not love that stems from that naivete. Not love, that stems from sorrow. Not the type of love that stems from low self-esteem. Not love that was not shown to them as a child. Not independent women who do not need a man or anyone. When everyone needs someone. You can be independent, but do we need to belittle our siblings to do that? We can all win together. We do not have to fight. We do not have to compete. There is enough success for everyone. But the devil has us believing that only one of us could win or be successful. I used to be like that. I thought that if a person is winning, that could never be me, or of course they are winning like a true hater. But God's vision for them is not the same vision that he has for you. Everyone you know can have the same passion, but our stories will be slightly different, and that slight difference is what will touch a whole other person's life. God needs all of us. In all our uniqueness, he wants us all to be successful. Just because someone else is beautiful does not mean you are not beautiful. You can both be beautiful. Just because that person wants to be with someone else does not mean you are not good enough. It means that you deserve to be number one in any relationship. And that is not the one. When I say number one, I do not mean over children or anything like that. I mean, the person God has for you will truly see you. They will see who you are. They will be attentive, and you will be worth the work necessary to feel special. That insecurity you feel if it is not due to a work that you still need to do on yourself is there because that person is not for you, and you might be forcing it. Even though it may be extremely hard, let

them go. I know you will feel lonely and missed some of their qualities. But imagine the best relationship you can hope for. Imagine the person you are with. Never forgets your birthday or holidays that are important to you. They speak your love language because they took the time to learn you. They give you flowers if that is your kind of thing or scalp massages. They believe in you. They cherish you. They are kind. They are understanding. They listen even when they are exhausted. They put in extra work to show you they care, and you listen, are attentive, and longsuffering you set standards and stick to them. You lift them without paying everything alone. You both have peace when you are together and that is all God. Please remember if you are ever unsure that "God is not the author of confusion" as TG Junior says. Anything that feels calm, peaceful, and loving now that is God. You can have that peaceful relationship. Do not listen to the people that say you have to settle to be disrespected. You are so much more than that and you deserve true love and happiness. Picture that peaceful relationship when you think about getting back into that unhealthy relationship because of the connection and time you had. It will give you some comfort when you start to feel alone. When you feel anger, hurt, disappointment and sadness, then get a hobby that adds to your personal growth and that business you have always wanted for yourself but could never do because the relationship took so much of your time. You can use it to that change the world and or your generation. Your child, your family, your community, and your friends are waiting on you to be who you were always supposed to be.

"Ye thou I walk through the valley of the shadow of death I will fear no evil for Thou art with me." Psalm 23:4

Chapter 13

Perspective

I realized that I used to listen to some irrelevant things and as I sat in my room listening to old shows and music I other songs that talked about being different and not conforming to the social norm, I noticed that a lot of the helpful songs were out there, but the bad outweighed the good. There were so many songs about disrespecting women, cheating, and smoking. I realized I was letting all of that into my system and I did not even realize it. I had been letting the low self-esteem sink in and every good message had Six bad, discouraging, self-doubting, and conceited or hateful messages instead of loving messages. I was learning from people who did not even know who were and I was thinking that they had everything figured out when they were just as confused as the rest of us. That is not to say that everyone does not have their own story, but even through your story, you should be willing to learn something and grow. I am not writing this as a judgment because God knows my mistakes were like a merry-go-round of me making mistake after mistake. I kept thinking I was doing the best I can and that was normal. But what was normal about settling and not getting what you truly deserve out of life. Everyone is on their journey and just because something is normalized does not make it right. There is so much more to life than half stepping into it. If life is short, why should anyone not want to live their life to the fullest? I mean, every breath, and every moment. No, every second that they have to the fullest. When you know life is not promised, why would you want to treat someone you love worse than most people treat their dog? Growing up I thought I was doing the best that I can, but if I am being honest, I was just confirming to fit in with everyone else. Through my relationship with Xavier, he would do things that I felt in my spirit were wrong. But my friends, some family members, and his friends were doing the same thing. I always thought I was wrong to disagree because it seemed like I was the only one that felt that way or that wanted a change in my circle. I did see a few Unicorn people like my mother who had standards and refused to lower them for anyone. Growing up everyone always thought my mom was beautiful and she was perfect to me. She is a smart, strong, and incredible woman, and when I thought of myself after the bullying, abuse, and negative self-talk, I always believed I did not deserve to have standards. When others thought that I was not even worth an unblemished life. I was so different, and I just could not imagine happiness, and fullness in my future. It made me feel unworthy of my standards, happiness, love, and encouragement. Whenever I set a standard and he would backslide or tried to go against me, it just reassured the little, insecure, abused child. It took forever to get myself on the right track. I had to have God pick me up off the floor and enter the people, material, books, events, videos, and music in my life to build me from the ground up. Without Jesus, there is no way I would have made it through, especially in the state I was in. When I first had broken up with Xavier, I was so weak that it took God himself to keep me going. I would have never made it through without him. It was His grace, His mercy, His strength, His power, His understanding, His everything that he gave to me so that I had the courage and the strength to become everything he always knew that I was even when I could not see it for myself. I had more in me than I could have ever dreamed of. God opened doors that he had to be there to open. Things just kept falling into place out of nowhere. I would think of something I would love to do and just like that I would be introduced to or bump into someone who had the connections that I needed to keep building my dream. I did not have to worry about money at all. I could just think about a bill

and my income, and my dad would randomly give me money, or I overpaid on a bill and would have more money, or people started to invest in me that believed in my gifts. It was not a huge investment, more like support, but it was everything that I needed. I would think about something I always wanted to do with my family, and it would happen. I would feel sad and ask God to take the pain for me and within a minute my tears would disappear, and I would feel full of the spirit of joy. I cannot explain everything that God did for me, but he saved me. If I were the old me, I would have never been so forgiving of Xavier and the hurt we caused each other. I had moments where I wished we could have been more mature and even different people. I think about my God, my peace, and my purpose and I know that if I was with Xavier. My relationship with God and my dreams would not have been as prominent as they are. I know that the hurt that I received from my relationship was familiar, but just because it was familiar does not make it right. You must start living the best life that you can because your purpose is waiting. So go for it.

Love is about more than just something that you see in the movies. Love is something that should be the guideline for success in any relationship. Love gives hope and peace to everyone. Love is the engine that helps each person drive through life. A car cannot go without love. The love that God has for us is what fueled Christianity and it can fill anything in life. God's love is what brought me through everything from my past and will continue to guide me into my future. Even when you feel your heart is broken, do not worry, because that heartbreak is one moment in time incomparable to a lifetime of blessings. I am not a perfect person and that is why God decided to use me. Sometimes when someone has been hurt badly, they see the change.

If you keep being a good person eventually that will help you grow into who you have truly become.

"Wherever we are, he sees us." John 1:50

Chapter 14
Emotional Trails

My emotions were constantly shifting like a car with a stick shift. I wanted to be OK so badly. I knew being without Xavier was the right decision, but that did not mean that I did not feel sad.

That did not mean that I did not get lonely, but when I got lonely, I felt God's presence. Sometimes I would feel myself losing control of my emotions and feelings as if I were losing my mind and all I could think of was God and ask him for his help and know he is God all by himself and even the mere murmur of his name in a state of weakness was enough to bring me from a stupor. That day, I kept getting flashbacks of my life with Xavier and him moving on with another relationship but laughing, being happy, and treating her the way he refused to treat me. It is not that I would not want Xavier to feel happy. I was just jealous. I was jealous and I felt like maybe if we changed the past and were different people, we could have made it work. I knew he was wrong for me. I knew I deserved better and yet still I missed him. I could not pinpoint a single happy moment with him or one moment that I felt actual love from him. Every time I thought back all I could imagine was how handsome he was, and my heart and soul could only feel a tug that felt like someone pulling put a lasso around my soul. The soul tie that we had was so strong. Most days I felt fine. I felt content and on other days I felt lonely and secure and as if I were losing something that was supposed to be my life but then I think back to not one single moment of happiness that was not followed by disappointment. I think about God's love. I think about how he wants me to be happy. I think about how he brought me out of that relationship. I think about the peace that came over me when I broke up with Xavier and forgave myself for any mistakes that I made in the past. I knew that I made the right choice, and unless God told me differently, I was going to continue to follow His word because He could not and would not steer me wrong. The devil tries to make a liar out of His word, but just the thought of my God brings me out of any sorrow, even amid disappointment. The Holy Spirit gives me a sense of calm and relief that I know could be nothing but God. If you trust and believe in his word, know that He is with you and He meant it when He said in His word that He will never leave you nor forsake you. He loves you.

Imagine your perfect life and God will give it to you and do time. And I promise what you receive when you trust and believe in him will be far greater than anything you could have ever dreamt of.

"Love is patient, love is kind. It does not envious, it does not boast, it is not proud." 1 Corinthians 13:4

Chapter 15
Out of my Hands

When I talked to Xavier. I felt like I was not in control, but God was. I saw what was going to happen before it did.

Not like Deja vu, but I could sense and hear God say, be kind, and asked Him to show me what to look out for. Having God in my life allowed me to see challenges before they exist. They are still hard challenges but having gotten there gave me provision before the test. God showed me skating with Xavier and him saying that he wanted to be with me. He showed the test before it was given. He knew that I would be weak, but having the answers made me feel stronger. I knew exactly what to look out for. It was like the devil was trying to trip me up or God was testing my obedience and He would not test me without first preparing me. Xavier, as I said before, was one of the best smooth talkers that I know who has ever walked on the face of the earth. He spoke things that I did not want to hear, along with things that I wanted to hear. I told him I needed to start over. He asked me what he would have to do for me to even consider giving him at least a date. We would need to start all over from scratch and I would need to be treated well/respected and he would have to come correct for me to even consider the possibility of a date. I needed him to work on himself for himself in his own time, and if he likes the way he is, that is fine, and I just wanted to put God first and respect. I wanted to be alone and work on being a better person. We both apologized and he listened to what I had to say, and I listened to him. After we talked, I went back through the things I said. There were some things I wish I did not say, but from day one when we met, I think I did exponentially better. I acknowledge my mistakes and listen to him talk. When he spoke some of the things he said unintentionally, helped me see where his head was. I wished I could have changed, who I was. But you cannot grow from perfection.

If or when God presented the men or man that he wanted me to be with, I wanted to love and honor him, and to be patient. I wanted to be ready. There was so much I needed to do before then. I needed to be the best person that I could be. I had to focus on my business and finish the projects that I wanted to complete. I needed to enjoy being single and then I wanted to meet the man that God always wanted for me.

I asked God what should I do if I stay? I feel insecure and like I am making the wrong decision if I go. If I stay, I feel the companionship and say I am okay with being treated as less than I should be. God said he will never change for you, but if you leave, he will change because of you.

I was floored. That is what I worried about. But if I loved Xavier, I knew he would be better without me. I needed to let him go. God said if I stay with Xavier, I will constantly protect him from the lesson that he is trying to teach him. I needed to remove myself so that God could reach him. At that moment, I felt clarity and I felt a push and pull. I wanted to move on, but it was not easy after all the time we had together and the soul tie that was created to just let go. I knew Xavier needed to be on his journey and learn what God wanted to teach him. But after the hurt that Xavier partially caused me, I felt sad and sorry for him because I could only imagine the hell, he would have to endure to see the pain he caused and appreciate his life. I felt so bad for him and the other person. Because it was different when you do not know better, and you make a mistake. It is worse when you know and hurt someone on purpose. You cannot tell God what to do and how to do it. I knew that I needed to listen to what God told me to do and focus on myself. I could not spend my life worried about when Xavier would grow and become better. I needed to be better and to do better. I needed to focus on the purpose, that God gave me. Focus on my relationship with God and be the best version of me I could be. I could not be my best self and harbor resentment, jealousy, and worry when I knew that God was about faith and hope. I did not think it would be so hard. People around me would say move on as I could just go to sleep and wake up emotionless. I knew I did not want to be disappointed by the same human more than once ever again.

    I just thought it would be easy. It did not help knowing I could meet a hundred men who would treat me better than Xavier used to treat me, or that I was getting asked on dates. It did not erase my emotions and knowing that Xavier would not treat me right. It did not erase my emotions. I mostly stayed clear of him, but it was so much harder when we had a child together. I wanted to just walk away and never see him again. I was bound to see him. I would release him and one sentence from Xavier would make my heart speed up. It is so hard to explain the control this man had over me. It was like I was focused on my life and doing all the things I could to heal, and I knew what I needed to do and the blessings that would be ahead of me. But because of the familiar

emotions and loving myself were new. It was like a comfort zone. I was so happy and peaceful with God and being alone. But I was so used to being in pain, hurt, and insecure. It made me feel crazy having real love. I know how crazy that must sound. There was a pastor that said, "it is like you are cheating on your future with your past"
and that is exactly how I felt.

As I sat there crying that day, thinking, why doesn't he love me? The one person that should only want me to spend and do life with me, but does not love me and God said as you love yourself? Do I love myself? Do I love myself enough not to settle? Do I know that I deserve better? Do I know that God wants me to feel loved, cherished, and honored? Do I know that I deserve love because God loves me and although I am unworthy, I know there is no reason that God will want me in pain over someone who does not see my value? It is easy to focus on one of the only men that does not want me or two, but what about the hundreds that do want me?

What about the people who God designed just for me? He made me to be someone's rib and if I were Xavier's rib, how could he turn his back on me? If he could not fight for me or us, then I know I needed to find someone who would. The pain and disappointment that I felt I would not wish on anyone. People around me say I should move on, and it should be easy, but it is not an easy feeling. The pain in your soul is ripping from your body repeatedly. A pain that is more unbearable than death. Not to discount the death of a loved one, but death gives you closure. A marriage torn apart is a continual pain that has no remedy but time. It has been nine months or so, and every time I feel fine out of nowhere, this pain hits me at random time periods. It keeps me feeling both sad and strong, like sadness is giving me strength when I should feel weak.

"No weapon formed against me shall prosper, And every tongue which rises against you in judgement you shall condemn. This is the heritage of the servants of the Lord." Isaiah 54:17

Chapter 16
Closure

When we signed the papers, I thought that I would feel relief or like a weight lifted from me, but I did not. I felt like I was losing my best friend.

Everything that we promised to each other the day that we got married was taken away from me and there was no way that I could get it back. If I could be in a relationship by myself, it would have lasted a lifetime, but being with someone else, it takes two people to make a relationship work.

Even when Xavier signed the papers, he looked hesitant, like he did not want to do it, but I did not know what else I could have done that would have changed the trajectory of our future. It seemed like I had done everything that I could to try to make the relationship work. But everything that I did was for not. All I wanted was my best friend back and to be treated with respect. I loved Xavier more than I ever loved anything in the world besides our child. Through all the self-love work I did for myself, and during my self-love journey I could not understand how I knew I was good enough and I deserved to be treated well, but Xavier did not understand or know that I deserve to be treated well. I deserved to be with him at his best or someone else who knew my value.

    I had a conversation with Xavier about how he regretted everything. He felt like he did not appreciate me when we were together. I felt the same way. Not just that Xavier did not appreciate me, but I never took the time to actually consider how Xavier felt in the situation. I was a horrible communicator. And when it came to listening to Xavier's opinion, I felt like I needed to prove that I was right.

    If you focus on your purpose God can handle the

rest. It is so easy in this life to doubt yourself, but do you not know that you are already where you need to be. I hope this book helps you walk into the life that God has always wanted you to have. The only person holding you back is you. You do not have to prove anything to anyone. You are not your past. You are not your

mistakes. You are who you were created to be.

    I know it may sound simple, but it is about so much more than proving if someone is right or wrong. I learned from a Bible Study class one day that sometimes we want other people to see our opinion. To see our point of view about a situation, but it is not someone else's responsibility to think exactly the way that we do. It is important to realize that just because you think differently than someone else does not mean that they do not love you or care about you. It just means that you are two totally different people and that is okay. When I was younger, before I started working on myself, I used to think. That. I needed to prove a point. I used to think that I needed to be right. I thought that my opinion was the only one there was. It is so funny how even when you think that you are done learning, you can always learn new things. Do not ever feel like just because someone has a difference of opinion that they are not hearing you. It is time for you to listen to them. Maybe it is time for you to listen to their point of view. If you just take a second and you listen to what they have to say, you may learn something about them that they were never prepared to share. Sometimes being so stubborn about wanting to be right will make someone else in their vulnerable state, shut down and not want to share things with you. We must be mindful that everyone is different because of their upbringing or because of their events through life or because of their personalities, or whatever it may be. So just because they do not see something the way that you do does not necessarily make them wrong or right and it does not necessarily make you wrong or right either.

 It is so weird how life goes. You could feel like. Everything is all figured out and then in the blink of an eye everything could change. It is so funny how I had wanted. For Xavier to acknowledge his part in everything and to do the work to be a better man, father, person, husband, and friend, but I had never considered him actually being able to change. I thought I had everything figured out. I had my mind made up. I knew what I wanted. I could not make a lifelong decision about my life amongst the opinion of everyone else. I needed to make a decision based on what I wanted out of my life. It is hard because when someone else decides your future for you, you do not have to feel guilty about making the wrong one. But when it is your time to make those big life changing decisions. It is only your fault if you make the wrong one. I would have to really been honest with myself and figure out what it is that I really want in my life. I know anyone reading this story is thinking it is too late. Xavier did too many things. We both messed up too much. We both did not lean on each other in the time where we should have been leaning on each other on a time where we needed each other the most. You are probably thinking if she decides to be with Xavier, she is making the biggest mistake of her life you're probably thinking. Why did I buy this book if all she is going to do is give me advice and then end up staying with some guy who did not appreciate her? You are probably even thinking what would make her share this part of the story with me when she could have just kept it to herself. I feel like transparency makes the best type of story that you could ever read. I cannot be honest about my opinion and then not be completely open about how I truly feel. It is never easy to say goodbye to someone, whether it is a good or an unhealthy relationship. It is normal to miss a person that you were in a relationship with for so long. It is normal to not have all the answers that you need. It is normal to want to be wanted by someone that you are in love with. It is even normal to follow your passion, to be a good person, and to be understanding to consider when the decisions you make and how they will affect everyone around you. Make that decision for yourself because you are the only one that can live your life. You know that old saying that if you try to tell God your plans, he laughs. I feel like this is so true because I thought I was done. I thought it was over. I thought there was no chance of any reconciliation. I felt like I was moving on with my life for the better and things would never be the same. I felt like I would never be the type of person that could ever forgive Xavier for any of the things that he did, but I also know that just because I forgave him does not mean that I need to give him another chance. That just means that I'm willing to stop carrying the burden of Xavier's mistakes and acknowledge the fact that this was a lesson that I needed to learn from. I am following God wherever he leads me whether it makes any sense or not. Some of the decisions or choices that I have to make in my life do not make sense, but I have peace about it. I feel like I am not just aimlessly wandering through life. I feel like I have a purpose and that my purpose is guiding me to where my destination is. In this process, I have been able to help so many women. I have been able to feel so free, so peaceful, and so joyous. I never imagined being able to have a day where I just took advantage of every single second, every single minute, every single moment that I was able to experience in my life. If I did not take a break from Xavier, if I did not start working on myself and I did not acknowledge what I did wrong and where I needed to start to grow, I would never become the woman that I am today. If Xavier and I were together it would only be God that held us together because it was His will. He could perform miracles for things only of His will. In my opinion, my life is God's will. Whatever he wants for my life, whatever he needs me to do and however he wants me to move. Wherever he needs me to go is where I will be. I am no longer selfish. I am no longer envious, or jealous or insecure. All of the security that I have ever needed is in God. All of the selfishness that I had now goes towards myself self-love. All of the envy I had is changed to motivation. I no longer have to feel insecure, because with God, I have so much security knowing that I can talk to and be with him whenever I need to. It is funny how so many people will try to feel a place in their heart with a hole in their spirit that cannot be filled by any other human being. Once you find God, He fills it up. He fills the hole with faith, with hope, with peace, and with prosperity. Everything that you need is in him. It is easy to do the wrong thing, but it is HARD to have a strength to be a better person.

I used to be afraid to ask for what I needed. I used to think that my problems were too small for him. But there is never anything that his child could go through that would be too small for him to help you through. You may be thinking, oh, this is just a little position that I want, or this is just a little strength that I need in this moment, or that this is just a little thing that no one else cares about, but He cares about us. He cares about every hair on our head. He cares about our well-being. He cares about our soul. He wants us to come to him whenever we have an issue. He is the one person that you can talk to about anything that will not judge you, that will help pick you up out of whatever stupor you are in. He will continue and continuously hold on to you even when
you feel like you are falling apart. He is the type of person that you can call on at any time of the day. You do not have to worry about him being tired or wiping crust out of his eyes or sounding groggy when you call on his name. All you must do is just stay in your word

and pray. And whenever you call whenever you need him, he will be there. He wants you to be Needy. He wants you to have a close relationship with him and to talk to him about whatever is on your mind. He is strong enough to handle any questions that you have, any doubts that you have, any struggles that you have. That is why He is

God.

"If God is for you no one can be against you."
Psalm 118:10

Conclusion

The breaking point is something that I had to go through to get to my strength. In a moment of weakness what clouded my mind was "Am I making the best decision, have I given this relationship everything that I got, was it as bad as I originally believed?

I wanted to believe in Xavier so badly that I completely neglected to let my common sense overcome any adversity that came my way.

I was so engulfed in the attraction, the lust, and everything superficial over substance, character, and mind. I wanted to believe that I was okay, but the moment I heard Xavier speak my mind, body, and soul crept back into the nativity that was every woman in love. It is so laughable that as a woman we can see the problems in every relationship except ours. We want to believe that our man is different, and give him the benefit of the doubt, but in the end, the only person that is receiving any spec of a benefit is the person we are in a relationship with.

Xavier was good. I felt things changing which is not necessarily a terrible thing as things would soon become final. I knew this day was coming, but I had no idea that I would react the way that I did. I felt like I was slowly losing myself again. There was only a mere atom sized chance that I would even be willing to hear him out. Specifically, what I needed Xavier to say, and I quote was." I will do anything that you need me to do just to get a chance to be with you and I will not make the mistake of hurting you again."

Even as I typed that last sentence in this memoir I laughed. I knew everyone besides me could see what was coming next and I knew I needed to keep my guard up because if I did not protect myself who was going to protect me but God. Something tugged at my soul when he said the words that I wanted him to say from the beginning. I wanted him to acknowledge the hurt that he caused as well. I knew there was a slim chance, but I hoped that would be a sign of his growth.

I was done with him and had to meet to get rid of a few of his things we talked about what it would take for me to consider giving him another chance to be in a relationship with me. I gave him the list. The list that I made when we were determining if we stood a chance against what came against us in the world. Over half of his message was perfect then out of nowhere he mentioned someone else and how great this person was. It was strange, to say the least, and something did not sit right in my spirit. I told him I needed to talk to him face to face to see what this was all about.

He tried to suggest we talk some other time, but there was no time like the present, and I had wasted enough of my life. It was now or never. I do not know what made me go there, I wanted to go home, but this nagging feeling kept pushing me in a direction I had only been once in our relationship. Upon arriving I asked

what was going on. He said we could talk. I asked if we could go inside, and he was with someone else. I did not scream, yell, or say any profane words, but the hurt I did feel.

This was his only chance and like always he blew it. I thank God that it did not take another 15 years to figure that out. It was precisely 22 hours, and my world was turned upside down. Stupid does not describe how I felt. I knew who he was, but like a moth to a flame, I still hoped that he had learned some things along the way and now knew my worth.

I had to go home to get ready for a virtual meeting and I did not want to blow up as I did in the past. I needed time to think to communicate the best way I could after cooling down. Xavier called every hour on the hour until I finally picked up the phone. I was so annoyed, and I felt defeated. In less than a day, Xavier managed to suck the life out of me.

I stayed calm when I answered, and I said everything that lay heavy on my heart. He tried to rebuttal but was told to be quiet by someone in the background. I told him his chances were over and I never wanted to talk to him again unless it involved business and that could be done via text message.

After speaking what was on my heart, I felt something that I can only describe as the presence of God. It was as if He were saying "I will never leave you nor forsake you"(Hebrews 13:5), what is done in the dark will be brought to the light (Hebrews 10:30) "no weapon formed against you shall prosper"(Isaiah 54:17), "you are strong"(John 2:14), "If God is for you who can be against you"(Romans 8:31). I felt like he was saying, "I brought you too far to leave you" (Philippians 1:6). He was saying that everything that I put inside you that I wanted you to give to the world that you lost before because you did not think you had it in you, I am giving it back. This breaking you just went through is given you the strength and the power that you need to encourage every woman who is like you, every woman who pushed someone away, every woman in a broken relationship, every woman who puts any man before God, any insecure woman, any woman who was bullied, any woman who did not believe in herself, any woman who did not know what red flags were will now have an inkling of what it may look like, any woman who is independent but needs inspiration, any women who do settle for less than God has for her, any woman who has heard warning from those around to leave that man alone but when she learned who he truly was had isolated herself because she did not want to hear the bad opinions about him, any woman who feels strong but never dealt with past trauma and it is affecting who she is in a relationship and with friends. This book is for every woman who is walking the earth.

As I am authoring the book, I feel like what can I say that has not been said. Even if I do not change the world, I hope to break the generational curse. I am so tired of fighting other women or seeing other women fight each other over a man, job, or opportunity that is for all of us to grab. If we work together in our relationship, we could change the world. I would love for love and kindness to change the world no matter how our opinions differ. You never know what someone else is battling or going through. Someone's bad attitude could be someone's struggle within themselves and has nothing to do with you. We are all on our journey. Remember you are enough because you were created by God. No one can change that. Remove toxic people out of your life and if you are toxic get help. Their struggle is not yours. Release anything that you cannot control from your mind. Resolve relationships that matter and that bring you happiness because they cherish you and you should cherish them. Lastly, recognize who you are and do not settle for anything less.

You Got This

Life is not a bed of roses, but God is everything that you need.

Book Club

1. What is the book about?

2. How did the book affect you?

3. Why do you think happened in the end?

4. What has been the pattern in your life?

5. What areas of the book can you relate to?

6. Where in your life have you seen glimpses of God?

7. Did Learn from my Missteps change any of your opinions about God or Christianity?

8. What were some of the things Learn from my Missteps teaches about God, faith, and life?

9. Would you recommend Learn from my Missteps to a friend?

10. Rate Learn from my Missteps on a scale of 1 to 5.

Red Flags

Add this after the story for book club and self-reflection or workbook that can be brought with or after the book.

Your Schedule

Set a schedule that keeps you on track during your healing process. Manage your time even with family and friends. Here is an example of mine.

Mental Timeouts

It is important to take 15 minutes to 1 hour to yourself to regroup, meditate, pray, and gather your thoughts so that you can add to the world.

Budget

Have a healthy financial budget.

You may feel like you want to splurge, but you cannot fix your soul with money.

Hygiene

From your breath to your skin. Find a self-care routine that can allow you to pay special attention to yourself.

Affirm yourself

You are your biggest fan. How can you expect someone to treat you better when you do not treat yourself well? This happens a lot with negative self-talk and the way you talk about others.

Standards

Stand for something or lay down for anything.

Examples:

    Standards: Caring, Patient, Consistent, Morals

    Dealbreakers: Bad Habits, Mental/ Physical Abuse, Inconsistency

Write your own:

    Standards:

    Dealbreakers:

My Quotes

When you dig deep and truly love yourself. Your standards change drastically.
- Trinesha

What are you afraid of? Do not be afraid to live life and love.
- Trinesha

Always acknowledge your wrongs so every day you can try to be better. Not perfect but better. Leading in LOVE.
- Trinesha

Give yourself the time you need to heal. We are so hard on ourselves trying to rush the healing process. Just because person A takes 1 week to heal does not mean you will heal in a week. Allow yourself the time whether that is 1 week or a few years. You deserve it. LOVE Yourself.
-Trinesha

It is time to do some self-reflection and LOVE Yourself.

Think about who you want to be, who do you see yourself as, and ask yourself are you proud of who you are?
- Trinesha

Take care of yourself so that you can help others. If you do not LOVE yourself, you cannot give real love to anyone else. That kind of love is dangerous, and you can feel like you are nothing without them. No matter who you are there is always 1 thing you can love about yourself. Hold onto that. You are enough and deserve real love.
- Trinesha

Focus on who you want to be. Be someone that you can be proud of by leading with kindness but always keeping your standards so no one can take your kindness for weakness.
LOVE Yourself so others know what to do.
-Trinesha

Not every day will turn out great, but every day can begin great with the right mind and a grateful heart. LOVE your life because no one is given the same path as you. Your gifts and dreams may be similar, but they are unique to who you are. We can all win.
-Trinesha

At times when you feel like you are alone. You are not alone. God is always with you. Make Him proud.
- Trinesha

Trust in Him and believe in yourself. When you start believing in yourself you become unstoppable.
- Trinesha

Every day when you wake up find 1 thing you are grateful for and try to find the good in everything just like you could find the bad in it. Your days will be so much better.
- Trinesha

Sometimes people may surprise you in the best way. Stick to your standards and love yourself so others have an appropriate example to go by.
- Trinesha
Do not settle to be treated with ignominy; you deserve

better. Know who you are and know your worth.

- Trinesha

Do not be anyone but you at your best; ever growing and ever learning. Lead with LOVE.
- Trinesha
Sometimes you just need to listen. You may have a lot of knowledge, but so does someone else.
- Trinesha

Let us start showing the people who deserve it our appreciation, so they know how grateful we are even when they are not requesting anything from us.
-Trinesha

When you start judging someone based on their heart vice their appearance you may be pleasantly surprised. The heart tells you everything you need to know about the character of any human.
- Trinesha

Sometimes you just have to stand up for yourself; respectfully.
-Trinesha

Lead with LOVE. Speak with kindness.

-Trinesha

Always remember who you are because there is a test around every corner.

- Trinesha

Mind/Heart

Lead with your mind and love with your heart.

Trinesha

Even when you feel lost fill your day with nothing but positivity until you find yourself again.

-Trinesha

Even in discomfort be who you are. If you are true to yourself, you can make the environment shape you.

-Trinesha

Sometimes it is hard to see the good during a bad time, but hope, gratefulness, and counseling can get you through.

-Trinesha

When you are blessed with something do not take it for granted.
-Trinesha
Live the life you want to live unapologetically. Always be humble with great character and wisdom. -Trinesha
Cherish the ones you love and appreciate everything that God has blessed you with.

-Trinesha

Think about it. What makes you? Is it a material item or person that makes you who you are? Who are you?

-Trinesha

Be kind to others. You may not control them, but you control yourself.

-Trinesha

Do not worry about what they think. What do you think about yourself? Are you working to become who you want to be?

-Trinesha

When I hear misery loves company there is no way that someone would want you to experience that type of sadness especially when you hope for the best for others. Be the best you no matter what.
- Trinesha

Do not be jealous be blessed. We all receive blessings. So be grateful and know your happiness is coming.

-Trinesha

Be kind not weak.

-Trinesha

Know that you are worthy even when you do not meet a goal.
-Trinesha

Do you know what I do when I am unsure...I stay still, I pray, and I ask God for guidance.

- Trinesha

The power of the tongue can make you become one within. Speak greatness over your life.

- Trinesha

Set your standards and do not change them for anyone or anything no matter how good it seems.

-Trinesha

Have resilience and be understanding.

-Trinesha

Keep standing up for yourself even when no one else will.

-Trinesha

What do you do when someone unintentionally breaks your spirit? For every negative thought say 2 scriptures or positive words.

- Trinesha

As long as you work hard your dreams will come true. You do not have to think outside the box. You are the box.

-Trinesha

Understanding possibilities will lead to your potential.

-Trinesha

Perfection does not exist. Be the best you and not anyone else.

-Trinesha

Even when you are in despair do not worry because there is happiness on the other side.

-Trinesha

Do not expect someone to be something that they are not but do expect God to be everything He promised He would be. -Trinesha

Know where you are supposed to be and go there.
- Trinesha

Help someone today, tomorrow, and every day. Your kindness will change your life and their life as well.

- Trinesha

Audacity over Pride & Ego

-Trinesha

Every act matters in life so take advantage of it.

-Trinesha

Knowledge is everywhere. Take what you need and use it to better yourself.

- Trinesha

You feel so confused when you try to do things your own way, but God is never confusing.

- Trinesha

Do not wait for tragedy, hurt, and pain to start living. Live the life God always intended for you.

- Trinesha

You are so exceptional. Expect everything you can imagine.

- Trinesha

Tomorrow says an affirmation and be kind to others even when they are not kind to you.

-Trinesha

Be Understanding of what others are going through, Righteous in your walk, and Kind to yourself and others.//
-Trinesha

Stop drifting and start living your life.

-Trinesha

Go forward with definite purpose.

- Trinesha

When you truly look at yourself through God's eyes you will start believing in yourself.

- Trinesha

Know your values, know your limits, and set boundaries.

- Trinesha

Imperfect, but perfect in the eyes of God. Be ever growing in your purpose.
-Trinesha
Love is much more than a feeling. Love is an action you show others by treating them with decency and respect.

- Trinesha
With so many blessings why would you want to be ungrateful?

-Trinesha

Do everything you can while you can.

-Trinesha

Know that your plans will change, but God's plan will not.

-Trinesha

You can say/do what you want, but the ultimate power belongs to God. -Trinesha

Earth is a spiritual warfare that can only be conquered through God.

- Trinesha

When u look around at your life and realize the peace u have comes from God and cannot understand being unappreciative. - Trinesha

I do not want to make ANY excuses for not doing what I want to do in life.

-Trinesha

We have so many bad examples of what not to do. Let us be long-tempered and an example we can be proud of.

-Trinesha

Take accountability, learn a lesson, stay prayed up, and stay blessed.

- Trinesha

Do not worry about what someone else thinks you are worth. Know what you are worthy of.

-Trinesha

I need Ruach Elohim(the Spirit of God) in my mind, body, and soul.

Breathing in the gospel.

-Trinesha

Think about what you want and how you plan to get it. No excuses and no doubts. Just believe in yourself.

- Trinesha

Do not spend your substance. Know your character and stand by it.

-Trinesha

Sometimes when I worry, I think why am I tripping when God got this.

- Trinesha

You are never really alone because God is there with you through sadness, happiness, and everything in between.
-Trinesha

Whenever you are questioning what you should do or conflicted ask God and He will give you the solution.
-Trinesha

Do not be afraid to ask for help. No one does it alone.
-Trinesha

Be about Kingdom work. We are so ready to put in that work, but would you be willing to have that same energy for God?
-Trinesha

How do we have time for greed, hate, and envy when it is better to forgive and love. Cherish your life.
-Trinesha

Some people will try to break you, but they will not because "no weapon formed against you shall prosper".
-Trinesha

Reap what you SOW. SOW into someone or something.

-Trinesha

Forgiveness is a strength. Holding a grudge is a weakness because you are not growing to your full potential.

-Trinesha

Forgive for yourself, learn for your growth, and understand for your wisdom.

-Trinesha

Who says we cannot change the world? The power of the tongue is undeniable.

-Trinesha

Life is not just about taking. Think about how you can serve others with no stipulations. You will be surprised.

-Trinesha

Choose to heal. Take as much time as you need because everyone heals in their own time.

-Trinesha

Why not you? Someone has to change things for the better. It can be YOU!

-Trinesha

We have so much potential waiting for us.

-Trinesha

God can fix any issue in your life.

-Trinesha

No problem is too big or small for God to handle.

-Trinesha

Keep your focus on God and he will do the rest.

-Trinesha

Never let yourself be put down by someone who is still finding themselves.

-Trinesha

Let us demolish Ochuroma (strongholds).

-Trinesha

Every day I feel blessed for everyone God entered into my life good or bad. The good keeps me thankful the bad teaches me.

-Trinesha

Do not stress it is just your amygdala.

-Trinesha

Twas the night before Christmas, and all through the house was love and God's grace as wisdom came from our mouths. God's vision of our lives danced in our heads. With execution and vision, our dreams were fed. Merry Christmas to all living anew. I wish you all the happiness as your dreams come true.
- Trinesha

It is the little moments that make the best memories.

-Trinesha

Listen. Learn. Testify. Repeat.

-Trinesha

The devil wants your guilt and jealousy. That is why selfless love, hope, and true happiness are so powerful.

-Trinesha

Forgive yourself for the things that you do not know and love yourself for the good decisions that you have made.

-Trinesha

We are all insecure but do not let your insecurity make you forget who you are and how you treat good people.

-Trinesha

Do not let spiritual warfare divide us from loving each other the way God intended us to.

-Trinesha

How can you expect others to change if you are judging them? Let it go so that you can grow.

- Trinesha

If you keep lowering your standards, you will end up on the floor instead of standing up for yourself.

-Trinesha
If something matters to you speak up, if not you are doing a disservice to them and yourself.

-Trinesha

Every day I am Makarios.

-Trinesha

Tomorrow is not promised.   Live out your life to the fullest. Appreciate every minute, every step, and every breath.

-Trinesha

Speak life into the ppl you love and around you. Every day we all have our own battles. It is time to change things. -Trinesha

Understand who you are so that no one can make you become something that you will never be.

-Trinesha

There is nothing like God's strength that brings you through every sickness and every situation in life.

-Trinesha

Breaking generational curses means more to me than my pride. Do not let pride keep you from growing.

-Trinesha

Sometimes we are in such a rush when God needs us here to humble us for where we are going.

-Trinesha

Follow your dreams and do not let fear stop you because God will take you the rest of the way.

-Trinesha

Isn't it amazing that we do not have to perfect, but just be obedient to be blessed and used for the purpose?

-Trinesha

When you surround yourself with respectfully Honest, Courageous, and Hopeful people you will succeed in

Jesus' name.

-Trinesha

I never want to be "so heavenly minded that I am no earthly good". -Trinesha

Put away pride to receive blessings.

-Trinesha

You can accomplish so much when God is with you even in the worst situation.

-Trinesha

Fear should not keep you from your purpose. Have faith.

-Trinesha

Stand for something and live in your purpose.

- Trinesha

When you know in your heart that Jesus is Love. You lead in Love instead of hate.

-Trinesha

God will fight battles for you that you do not even know exist and use you no matter who you are or what you have been through

-Trinesha

We need to do better because we CAN be better.

-Trinesha

God saw something in me even before I ever knew there was anything there.

-Trinesha

Reflect before you react. Be selfless and uncontentious so you can look back & know you did everything at your best.

-Trinesha

Listen even when you disagree you may learn something new.

- Trinesha

When I am weak God is strong.

-Trinesha

Even when God shows you what you are about to go through you cannot prepare for it, but He will be right there.

-Trinesha

Repudiate anything that is below what God says you are worth.

-Trinesha

Nothing that I go through in life is ever going to make me stop praising His name.

-Trinesha

God is love. Love yourself so that you can give the love you want to receive.

-Trinesha

No matter who you were in the past God can use you going forward.

-Trinesha

You do not have to be perfect to live in the purpose God gave you. You just have to be willing and obedient.

-Trinesha

Even when it is hard, you have to stick to your standards. The blessings on the other side will amaze you.

-Trinesha

Love who you are at this very moment.

-Trinesha

Pray for those even when they look happy. Sometimes happiness is a mask of despair.

-Trinesha

Be patient when you are in your waiting season because your blessing is coming.

- Trinesha

You do not have to fit in because of the choice being a majority vote. Sometimes standing out is what really matters.

-Trinesha

Do not allow a stumble to make you to fall.

-Trinesha

Sometimes we have our hand out instead of holding out our hand. -Trinesha

Do not let anyone pull you out of purpose by distraction because they cannot see the vision behind what God called you to.

-Trinesha

How many resolutions did not last? Just because you stumbled does not mean it is time to give up.

- Trinesha

Sometimes when life tries to bring you down you just have to take a moment and sit under the fig tree.

- Trinesha

You are not a superwoman. You have God. Lean on Him.

-Trinesha

Revenge is not something you have to seek. Pray for others and let God touch their hearts.

-Trinesha

Keep moving forward even when you do not see a change because you will look back and be amazed at how far you have come.

-Trinesha

Let go of your past mistakes because God has already forgiven you and is waiting on you.

-Trinesha

Do not let mercurial emotions cloud your judgment.
-Trinesha
When good things happen to you accept it because you are only neglecting your blessings when you do not.

When you feel confused about the next step be still and wait for God's instruction because He is building you.
-Trinesha

Let others be who they are. Sometimes we want others to be just like us, but they cannot because God made us all different.
-Trinesha

Be careful what you speak over your life. Start leading with love and speak life into your vision and into your dreams.
-Trinesha

Do not spend so much time worrying about the future that you do not enjoy the day that God has given you.
-Trinesha

Honor what God is doing in your life right now.
-Trinesha

Sometimes when God has created a vision for your life the only thing stopping you is you.
-Trinesha

-Trinesha

Honor God, lead with love, stay focused, dream big, and inspire others.

Trinesha

Before you lead ask God for direction so that you do not end up going the wrong way.

-Trinesha

Acknowledge your accomplishments and be grateful because no one was created like you.

-Trinesha

Sometimes being a good listener tells you everything that you need to know.

-Trinesha

There is no comparison to God's plan.

-Trinesha

I cannot, I will not, I do not... April Fools, "I can do all things through Christ who strengthens me". Phil 4:13

-Trinesha

When no one is listening remember that God is.

Be patient and take your time because your help is on the way.

-Trinesha

You cannot fix every problem. Just pray.

-Trinesha

When you think about your actions think about how you want to present yourself. What do you want your name to mean?

-Trinesha

Being surrounded by people who support and push you forward is so important.

-Trinesha

Persistence with God can overpower any enemy.

-Trinesha

Just because you cannot always get what you want does not mean you will not get what you need.

-Trinesha

-Trinesha

When you have no faith, you leave no room for the mustard seed to grow.

- Trinesha

Do not doubt what God has called you to because it was never done the way that you are doing it.

- Trinesha

Do not let someone's insecurity tell you who you are.
Trinesha
Protect your purpose and open your heart.
-Trinesha
God is with you every step of the way. He will be there no matter where you are or who you are.

-Trinesha

Do not tell God no because you will take a long way and end up where you should have started.

-Trinesha

Once you start believing in yourself it makes doubt cease to exist.

-Trinesha

Sometimes you have to just say yes to things in life even when you are scared. Uncomfortably is growth.

-Trinesha

Appreciate everything even the small things.
It is time to come to God. Lean on Him. It does not matter what you have been through or what you have done.

-Trinesha

Understand obedience and let His will be done.

-Trinesha

Procrastination is the enemy's ammunition. We pull the trigger on the weapon that carries the bullet that stops our purpose.
-Trinesha
If the devil is trying to stop your purpose, you know it is something big.

-Trinesha

It is easy to be ungrateful when you are not thinking about all of your blessings.

-Trinesha

Do not let distractions keep you away from your destiny.

-Trinesha

-Trinesha

If we know life is precious, why are so many of us taking it for granted? -Trinesha

When you seek God, sin never looks the same.

-Trinesha

Quiet your tongue and let your mind listen.

-Trinesha

As long as you take responsibility for your actions you are already on the right track.

-Trinesha

Release everything that does not serve you.

-Trinesha

Obedience to God can break any stronghold.

-Trinesha

Wisdom just commands that you listen.

-Trinesha

It is okay if you fall, just call on a wise friend and pick yourself back up.

-Trinesha

You can try to do everything right and still make a mistake. It is not about solecism it is about your intention.

-Trinesha

Do not worry about trying to be accepted by everyone else because God already accepts you.

-Trinesha

Do not get so lost in what you are missing that you forget all that God brought you through to make it to this point.

-Trinesha

Remember to hold yourself accountable & get an accountability partner for ur life goals a Family member/Friend/Life Coach.

-Trinesha

Your mind, body, and soul are not a game.

-Trinesha

It is easy to complain when you are not thinking about your blessings.

-Trinesha

Seek God 1st before you make any decisions. We do not have time to waste.

-Trinesha

Sometimes we spend so much time focusing on hate, and

politics that we forget that God is greater than everything.

-Trinesha

Start being intentional about your life. You are only cheating yourself.

-Trinesha

Keep your hands held high (praise), your feet standing strong (standards), and your tongue with wisdom (power).

-Trinesha

If you fail a test from the adversary take notes so you know what to do the next time. Breathing=another chance

-Trinesha

You are worthy of the purpose that God has given you. Stop doubting yourself.

-Trinesha

If someone is not against you, let them be them because even something against you does not stand a chance.

-Trinesha

Low standards prevent you from reaching your purpose.

-Trinesha

When your past tries to define you, it is up to you to remind yourself of where you are going.

-Trinesha

Trust Him. Trust His timing and His word. He will give you things that you did not even know you needed.

-Trinesha

It is not about you; your purpose should change things.

-Trinesha

Instead of judging others, what if we prayed for them and asked if they are, okay?

-Trinesha

Take care of yourself so you can be better for those around you.

-Trinesha

About the Author

Trinesha Catrell

I am an entrepreneur, author, and speaker. Born and raised in a household with two business-minded parents, by the age of 15 I knew that I was created to help others. That is how my passion for motivating others arose and since then, I gained knowledge in this field due to real life experiences.

On my journey to self-love and self-development, I learned a few very significant things. I put God first in my life because He is everything to me. He gave me strength when there was nothing left. I acknowledge that I am not perfect, but I always strive to be a better person. I love myself because God created me, and I choose to help others as they journey through their life.

The rose symbolism signifies the special love that God has for human beings. Also, it signals holiness, and the rose is the attractive center point that can help make life more meaningful. So, it shows the love that persists and the control of every step that follows in your duty.